ADVANCE PRAISE

"Written with compassion and wit, propelled by a daughter's need to know, *Eighteen for Life* bears firsthand witness to the unfathomable inhumanity of the Holocaust while unravelling family mysteries taken to the grave. It's a quest that becomes a celebration of life lived against the odds, the power of art to process the past and, through it all, the stubborn, sometimes painful persistence of love."

–Diana Wichtel, author of award-winning *Driving to Treblinka*

"The memory lives on" (cast glass, candles), installation at "Eighteen for life, ten to remember" 2002 (Photo: Haru Sameshima)

EIGHTEEN FOR LIFE

SURVIVING THE HOLOCAUST

HELEN SCHAMROTH

ISBN 9789493418271 (ebook)

ISBN 9789493418257 (paperback)

ISBN 9789493418264 (hardcover)

Publisher: Amsterdam Publishers, The Netherlands

info@amsterdampublishers.com

Eighteen for Life is part of the series *Holocaust Heritage*

Cover image: Martha and Feliks with Helen, Cracow 1946.

CONTENTS

1. Freedom 1
2. Gift 9
3. Gefilte fish 15
4. Stains 19
5. Eighteen for life, ten to remember 27
6. Talking funny 35
7. The Best 44
8. Courage 53
9. Having Babies 71
10. Once was a family 83
11. Gambling 89
12. Don't tell me what you can't do 101
13. The queue 108
14. Another world 119
15. Secrets and half truths 129
16. Violets and lily of the valley 139
17. On the run 156
18. A story to be told, again 166

Photos 187
Acknowledgments 203
About the Author 207
Amsterdam Publishers Holocaust Library 209

'Eighteen for Life' is dedicated to the memory of my parents, Martha and Feliks Ash.

My mother would say, "I will take secrets to my grave."
My father would say, "I don't want you to think I was a hero."

The challenge for me and my sister as the second-generation survivors was to discover what they were talking about.

1

FREEDOM

Lvov 1945

Loud drunken men in Russian uniforms jostled her. Pfe. Disgusting uneducated pigs, Martusia muttered under her breath as she tried to hide her revulsion of their stench, of their lewd taunts and the way they undressed her with their eyes. She pushed her way through the carriage in a vain effort to find a seat, hating how her breasts were handled like bread dough. So humiliating, yet she knew it would be worse if she said anything.

The train lurched forward. For a moment she shut her eyes. Strong arms caught her as she started to fall. Someone found her a seat, a bottle was pressed to her lips. She took tiny sips, willing the vodka to taste like soup.

"Bread, please," she whispered hoarsely in Russian.

Her savior shrugged. "There is no food. Here, drink. Drinking helps me forget. And I need to forget."

Me too, she thought as painful memories struck like poison-tipped darts.

The journey from Lvov took many hours, and her mood softened as the liquor and flirtatious banter worked on her. She found herself wondering whether this soldier might help her. Not without expecting favors in return, she was sure.

The soldier assured her he could find her somewhere to stay in Crakow, and he would get some food for them both. She didn't really believe him but the fantasy helped to pass the time. She leant back, thinking about Felek as she dozed off.

When she first met Felek, not a lot impressed Martusia except for his *chutzpa* and the way his eyes smiled when there was little to smile about. They were two solitary people, the only ones now left of their families. He was talkative, persuasive, and he promised to keep her warm and safe. She resisted at first. But then she married him.

Within a few months, six long years of war had ended and Felek was anxious for them to move away from war-ravaged Lvov and the memories that haunted them. He would go ahead to Crakow, find somewhere to live and work, and send for her as soon as possible. Meanwhile she should continue working for the Russians.

Three weeks passed and Felek sent word with a friend that he had established a small business in Crakow, buying cardboard boxes and selling them to fledgling enterprises. She should join him soon and, in the meantime... a present – a new hat. She appreciated her husband's kindness, if not his taste. Before long the Russian supplies office where she worked closed down abruptly, so there was every reason to go and find Felek.

They reached Crakow and the train braked abruptly. She sat up with a start. Soldiers with guns slung carelessly over their shoulders spilled onto the platform, and she tripped in the crush. Her knee was grazed, her new hat crumpled. All she could do was burst into tears as she scrambled to her feet. Anxiously she touched her belly.

Light was fading and a cold panic gripped her. When the crowd at the station thinned, she saw two women and a child further along the platform. They seemed as bewildered as she was, and they held their meager possessions in small battered cases close to their bodies – just as she did.

Beyond tears, beyond pride, the older woman turned to a soldier and in Yiddish-tinged Russian begged for a coin so that she might buy some bread for her small daughter. Martusia recognized the soldier who had shown her a moment of kindness on the train and she watched him turn to casually flick a few sparkling coins in her direction rather than to the other women.

Callous bastard, she wanted to shout as she scooped them up. It was tempting to keep the money but she heard her mother's words, always urging her to share her good fortune, however meager.

She walked over to the trio. The emaciated child stared at her through dark-rimmed meerkat eyes. In her slightly delirious state – had she drunk too much vodka? – she wondered if the child knew what a meerkat was. She remembered walking with Felek, how he talked about his childhood and the animals at the Warsaw Zoo, and the funny meerkats. She must be going mad. Who thought about meerkats when all she should really think about was not having any food – which was definitely not funny.

"Madam, perhaps we could find somewhere to eat," she suggested in Polish. "Do you mind if I walk with you?"

The woman nodded and introduced herself, her sister and her shy daughter.

Images of food and shelter danced in front of them like *dybbuks* – the ghostly spirits of Jewish folklore – and Martusia wondered where they were being led. Suddenly, a door burst open and a group of men, reeling and singing, caused them to step back into the shadows of a doorway. They waited for the raucous sounds to fade and continued, they hoped, towards the town center.

Eventually they paused in front of an elaborate wooden door, where a light shone through a small window, and a sign by the door suggested it was some sort of guest house. A tiny, discolored pencil-shaped patch at a jaunty angle and two tiny nail holes indicated that a *mezuzah* had been torn from the doorpost.

Martusia's pregnancy made her feel sick, even with no food in her stomach; her feet and back ached and she felt unable to walk much further. Her companions were equally exhausted. And cold. All the same it took courage to knock on the door. They were a bedraggled lot, huddled outside the doorway. The child wrapped herself tightly in her mother's skirt, as if afraid to show her face. Martusia was trembling slightly as she approached the burly man who filled the doorway. He sported a mop of greasy, graying hair and she was relieved to see that his red face was not unkind. At first not a word was spoken.

Eventually she held out most of the coins. "Please... please can we have some food... and a bed?"

The man pocketed the money, grunting. "It's not really enough for so many of you," but he moved aside to let them in. Once inside they stood absolutely still, like exhibits in a museum. Six pairs of male eyes bored into them and steam rose from a pot on a grate over a fireplace at the far end of the room. "Okay," he muttered before resuming his card game.

A young woman wearing ragged but clean clothes picked up some bowls, and called cheerfully, "Come and eat. You look hungry."

The hubbub resumed.

The woman's kindness and the warmth in the room made Martusia's eyes sting. She sank onto a wooden bench and slowly pulled off her gloves. The first spoonful was heaven – the thickest, tastiest potato soup she had eaten for a long time. She tried not to eat too quickly and urged the others to take care so as not to upset their stomachs.

There was a double bed in the back room, covered with a yellowing quilt, feathers escaping from its seams, and topped by two flat square pillows. Worn brocade, in what were once rich warm colors, partially covered the bed, indicating a glamorous previous life. Beside the bed was a stained, chipped chamber pot, which thankfully was a whole lot cleaner than the toilet they had used.

The three women and the five-year-old girl pulled off their worn boots and fell onto the bed fully clothed. Martusia lay awake and listened to the rhythmical breathing of her companions. They were out of time with the scratch, scratch, scratch of rats nearby. After some time she slipped into a fitful sleep.

Early in the morning she moved out quietly.

A small hand slid into hers. "Stay with us," the child pleaded. "Mama and Aunty are so scared and you could help us."

"I must go," she whispered, embracing the little girl and kissing her forehead. "I need to find my husband."

Her breath billowed white clouds in the early morning air and she pulled her coat around herself more tightly. Her gloves were falling apart at the seams and her hands were soon like ice. Instinctively she walked towards the center of the city. All she could think of was where she might find something to eat. At the same time she couldn't help noticing what a beautiful city Crakow was. What's more it looked like it hadn't been bombed.

Her early morning optimism started to fade when the cup of tea her last tiny coins bought warmed her but did nothing to fill her stomach. Salty tears fell into her tea. Where was another meal, another bed, and how would she find Felek?

She wandered into Rynek Główny, the town square, thinking about her husband. Ach, coming to Crakow was such a stupid thing to do. She leaned against a wall and slumped onto her small suitcase that held everything she owned and sobbed quietly, not caring that people were looking at her. She had yearned for freedom and peace for so long, yet she didn't know how to rid herself of the fear in her stomach or the thumping behind her eyes. She couldn't remember what it was like to feel safe or to trust anyone. Where could she find a small calm oasis?

Suddenly she straightened up, not believing her eyes. There he was! Strolling into the square! Walking arm in arm with a young woman to whom he was talking animatedly. Martusia was conscious of her grubby appearance and tear-filled eyes. She felt embarrassed.

How could he? Was this the freedom she prayed for when she married him, the security, the better life – after all those horrific years? For a terrible moment she wished she had miscarried his child. How could she have survived a war only to experience such betrayal and humiliation? The worst moments of her life flooded back... losing her first husband... her mother's last words...

Her pain quickly turned to fury. *Oh no*, she thought as she stood up and smoothed her coat. She hadn't survived just to give in to a bitch wearing such a terrible hat and too much lipstick. Martusia strode across the square. "Felek," she called.

He looked across to her and his face turned beetroot red. "Tusia, I can't… I can't believe that you are here. When did you arrive?"

"My darling, I couldn't wait when the Russians closed the office and there was no work anymore." She walked up to him. "Feel our baby. Our new life," she said, placing his hand on her slight roundness. "We needed to be with you. And who is she?" she spat as the other woman stalked off.

"Nobody who matters my darling. I missed you. Come, let's eat something."

"Yes please. I am so hungry."

The story of my mother leaving Lvov for Crakow was one that evolved over the years, and as memories do, each version produced a slightly different picture. As I recall, the older I got, the more details she added, but it was essentially the same story of her, a pregnant woman, alone, leaving by train. It was a story she was happy to share.

Recently I delved into the tapes recording her life, as told to an interviewer. It never occurred to me that I would find a very different version.

In early 1945, it wasn't possible to move from city to city without a travel permit in what was then under Russian occupation. Martusia managed to acquire a permit and was contemplating how to get from Lvov to Crakow when, two days after getting her permit, she encountered a friend of Felek's. He had arrived in Lvov by truck and was carrying a lot of German marks from Felek for her, as well as an address for him. This was a relief for her, but then, the day she received the money was the very day the currency was devalued and became worthless. Which left Martusia with little money as she was no longer working for the Russians.

She was able to borrow some money and got together with a small group of people who also wanted to leave Lvov. They carried a mattress and a few personal belongings, and for a couple of days they would go to the main road and stand shivering as they waited for a truck. At the time Martusia's pregnancy was making her really sick, and she vomited day and night.

Finally, they found someone with a truck and set off, thinking they would get to Crakow within the day. It was freezing cold and there was a snow storm. The truck broke down in the snow and the Russians who owned the truck could do nothing more than swear as they had no idea what to do. There was no food, only vodka, and all Martusia wanted to do was to pull down her breeches and urinate in the field when she wasn't vomiting.

It was a relief when a Polish policeman arrived from a nearby village and led the men in the group to find some straw for bedding. They had a terrible night and the next day while the Russians managed to repair the truck with assistance from locals, the policeman took the group to his mother, in the hope that she could help. This kind woman found an egg, a bit of flour, salt and two potatoes. Martusia was grateful that she had learned to cook as a child, and she mixed the egg, flour, salt and water, kneaded and stretched the dough, and cut rounds using a glass rimmed with flour. She cooked the potatoes, mashed them and made *piroshkes* – parcels of soft pastry filled with potatoes and cooked in salted boiling water. It was a feast, hot food after their ordeal, accompanied by a glass of milk provided by the policeman's mother.

The truck eventually arrived in Crakow after curfew and the group of eight people was unceremoniously dumped in the center of the city near a hotel, where soldiers immediately surrounded them, not allowing them to move. After some negotiation, the group – cold, filthy, with snow on their boots – was permitted to move into the hotel.

It was a couple of days before Martusia found Felek – he had moved out of that very hotel a day earlier. And then he appeared. With another woman on his arm.

To this day I am mystified as to why there are two versions – each equally plausible.

2

GIFT

Lvov 1944

Martusia had been hunched over a typewriter, pecking at the keys – not very expertly, she would have been the first to admit – when an unexpected gust of October air stabbed her. She was sitting at what passed for a desk – an old door covered with paint smears, balanced on a rickety frame – and she was perched on an uncomfortable slatted wooden stool. She looked up cautiously.

"Good morning, madam. I need to talk to somebody, to your boss. I need work, money, zlotys," said the man. "I'm hungry."

His clean clothes, at least two sizes too big, danced out of rhythm with his stride as he moved towards the desk, his trousers dragging along the ground. He spoke a mixture of Polish and Russian, overlaid with a Yiddish accent.

"Get out," she hissed. "They will kill you."

Through nights when he ached, he had dreamed of women of such beauty – women with blond curls, piercing blue eyes and a pale complexion, like hers. The visions had helped to block out fearful nights after endless days. Days spent shoveling decaying bodies... Days spent extracting gold teeth...

There were other visions: a pair of dark-skinned beauties... a bevy of golden-haired goddesses. The women in his dreams had smiled and flirted. They fed him grapes... tropical fruits... made love to him.

And here was this rather anxious woman with her flawless Polish, seeming to be concerned about his safety.

"They kill Jews," she snapped.

He gestured towards the inner office. "I must have work to live."

Martusia prayed that he would be turned away.

After more than 15 minutes in her superior's office the man reappeared, laughter in his eyes. A short dour uniformed Russian, whose jacket was belted tightly over his well-fed belly, trotted behind him.

"This is *Pan* Felek Ash. Please meet *Pani* Martusia Wagner. He will be your supervisor," said the Russian.

"Oh really. Thank you so much." She flashed a smile that lasted just until the Russian left.

"Uneducated idiot," she threw quietly in his direction.

Evening. A shadowy figure emerged from the darkness, footsteps crunching what was left of the crumbling pavement. "Walk with me," said Felek, offering his arm. "Nothing more. It will be safer for you."

"Please go away," she begged. "They have no idea that my identification papers are false. Please don't spoil it for me."

He looked surprised at her admission. Was this gorgeous woman who looked like a *shikse* Jewish?

"And don't think the Russians are so much better than the Germans. No one is safe."

He shrugged and they walked carefully, negotiating mounds of stones and splintered wood which had once been beautiful buildings that had lined the street. The stench of rubbish, death and decay saturated the air, and their clothes. Sounds of gunshots and tanks grumbling over cobblestones were fortunately some distance away.

Despite the depressing environment, Felek launched into talking about the wonderful life he imagined he would have one day, taking trips to visit the South Sea islands of his dreams and the beautiful home he hoped to own. It would be far, far away, at which point Martusia smiled. Who wouldn't want to be far away from this war-torn place?

He raced backwards into stories about the Warsaw yeshiva of his youth and the wonderful meals his mother used to cook. He salivated as he described the salty jellied *gefilte* fish they ate for Shabbos and festivals, and the fluffy Pesach *kneidlach* – those delicious soft matzah balls that floated in soup. They were his mother's specialty. And hers was the tastiest chopped liver cooked to perfection, studded with onion fragments that had been fried in salty *shmaltz* – the creamy chicken fat that had been pulled from the inside of the raw chicken and melted, leaving glorious brown crunchy pieces in a bed of fat. The whole lot was best eaten spread on thickly sliced rye bread. And of course, there was always golden chicken soup loved so much by the family, often with creamy strands of egg swimming through it like tadpoles.

Stories of his parents, two sisters, two brothers and a baby niece quickly followed – all brutally killed. And his distraught wife who had taken a cyanide pill before she could suffer like the other women who were taken away. He paused.

Martusia couldn't help admiring the spirit of this gaunt man with his prematurely receding hairline, a man who had lost so much. It was hard to understand how he could be so optimistic and how his ever-laughing dark brown eyes showed little evidence of what he must have gone through. He seemed kind, and she believed him when he said that he knew more about making shoes than managing a supplies office.

"So where have you been until now?" she asked quietly.

Felek stared ahead, eyes misting, and they walked more slowly. Suddenly he spat out the answer, like rotten meat. "The *Toten Brigade*, the Death Brigade at Janowska camp! Not so far away from here. It was the worst smelling hellhole on earth.

"You know, 134 of us... we broke out of that place. Some were shot when they came out... some got out... Who knows how many of us are still alive." Silence. He smiled at her through his tears. "I think I am the luckiest man to be alive. Now every day is a gift."

Every day after work Felek walked with Martusia. She told him about Zloczow, her home town not too far from Lvov, and her widowed mother who never remarried. Her aunts, her uncles. And her husband. All dead.

"I've lost everyone, my mother and my husband were shot in the same week, more than two years ago. And I never knew my father who died when I was a baby."

"Marry me," he said after a week passed.

"You must be crazy."

But she continued to walk home with him. He told her how he was keeping warm at night, huddled between two others who had escaped with him, men who shared his wage and a tiny room with one mattress. But soon there would be a bigger room with space for her, he promised. And gazing at her, he admitted that he thought more about her than about his stomach pangs.

A month passed, a month of wind that raced through buttonholes and temperatures that froze the dampness between threads.

She thought about the cold little room she shared with four women. "All right. I'll marry you. Promise me you will keep me warm."

She wondered if this was madness when he kissed her tenderly, a little clumsily. It was an effort for her to dismiss memories of the tall, good-looking, well-educated man she had loved so passionately, and lost. But this was wartime, when people drank watery soup, broke their teeth on stale bread and froze to death.

They married. Twice. The first time in a registry office, on Felek's birthday, cost three *rubles*, with strangers as witnesses. Not long after, Felek met a rabbi who had been friendly with his father. The rabbi had miraculously survived, but not so his loved ones. He was pleased to marry them properly under a *chuppah* – a piece of white cloth Martusia got from her boss at the supplies office. Felek borrowed money to pay for the wedding.

A friend offered Martusia some tulle that had been a pram cover. She transformed it into a veil to cover her face as was Jewish tradition. Scraps of white lace became a blouse, a wide ribbon became a bra under it. They found old friends, and there were new friends who all helped to make the wedding possible.

It was late November and freezing cold on the morning of the wedding. Martusia was running late for work, lateness being treated very seriously by the senior manager. The wedding was to be held in their apartment and in her hurry to heat the room before she left, Martusia struck a match directly to the gas pipe rather than to a piece of paper first. Fire caught her hand and her sleeve which required a detour to a chemist. It made her late for work, fortunately with no penalty when her boss saw her burned hand. But as a result, it was impossible to put the wedding ring on her finger.

After the ceremony, with a wry look, Felek handed Martusia a gift that belied his Orthodox upbringing, a gift he had managed to buy on the black market.

"One day", he said, "we will have a life of real luxury, like this. And more. All the time."

It was the most seductive, extravagant gift. A generous man, she thought, and she so appreciated it. She held back just long enough to thank him, then attacked the pair of heavy, dark slabs of buttered rye-bread which enclosed a thick slice of pink ham edged with creamy fat. Who would have believed that she could enjoy it so much? Maybe... maybe life could be worse.

Melbourne 1963

"Helen," called Dad. (He always pronounced it 'He-wen', as if it was written in Polish.) "There is a telephone call for you." My date was going to be late. Would he arrive with chocolates or flowers this time? Always generous was a plus, my father told me.

"Hey Helen, is your boyfriend Jewish?" my little sister Evie asked (she became known as Eve in adulthood, but stayed Evie forever for some family friends).

"Yeah. Anyone I go out with always has to be Jewish, preferably aiming to be a professional man, if I'm prepared to let them into the house."

"You're kidding!"

"It's just too excruciating if they aren't. Mum once suggested I meet them at Uni, to avoid Dad freaking out. I can't believe that at my age they still monitor who I go out with."

"That's ridiculous."

"I wasn't much older than you are when I asked if it was going to be okay to go out with someone who wasn't Jewish. Mum was good about it and she wasn't too worried, which makes me think that she must have gone out with plenty of non-Jewish boys. Maybe it was just luck that she married a Jew. But Dad freaked out."

"Well, I want to ask her about how come they sent me first to a Baptist school, then a Church of England school when we moved to East St Kilda. The Baptist school sort of made sense when you didn't speak English and they had to find a school that would accept you. But I've always spoken English, and they didn't choose Mt Scopus, the Jewish school for either of us. And how come Dad was so old when they got together?"

"Hang on with the questions Evie. Don't go there. Please. Dad had one of his terrible headaches after I asked about going out with non-Jewish boys. I don't want that on my conscience again. I honestly can't understand how come he's so stuck in that Orthodox mindset, even when he doesn't live that way anymore. I mean, as long as I can remember we've had oysters and ham in the fridge."

"And crayfish. Yum," Evie giggled. "And he works on Saturdays. For someone who used to be very religious when he grew up, he's done a big flip. I wonder why?"

I paused for a moment. "Dunno. I reckon he was still essentially Orthodox during the war, in his mind at least. He said his father would appear in his dreams and tell him Talmudic stories. And apparently his Dad had wanted to be a rabbi but needed to earn a living to support his family. After all, there were five children."

"I'm glad we're not so religious and kosher, but I wonder why? I'm gonna ask Dad that too."

"Hm. You'll have to pick your moment."

3

GEFILTE FISH

Brussels 1947

Steam wafts from the cooking pots and the fishy smell makes Martusia feel light-headed. The kitchen feels crowded with Felek's relatives busy cooking. It's been more than six years since she's seen so much food in a kitchen. Six years of nightmares. Not just nightmares. Six years of vicious reality. Six years of war – of hell, loss, pain and so much hunger.

One of the women tries to remove the slippery fish heads from a deep pot without burning herself. "Martusia, please help me," she calls in French.

Martusia obliges. The eyes of the cooling carp cloud over and jelly starts to form on the plate. She runs her finger over the edge of the dish the way she did as a child, and licks it. The taste isn't quite right.

The voices of the women float over her as she remembers the kitchen of her childhood in Zloczow.

She had often cooked with her mother. One day, when she was about nine, her mother was holding a ball of minced fish and trying to wipe her nose with the back of her hand.

"Tushinka, please find my handkerchief and wipe the fish off my face for me. I will smell of carp forever if I leave it."

Martusia dug deep into her mother's pocket searching for the embroidered square that was always to be found there. Solemnly she patted her Mama's face, trying not to laugh at the sight of her elegant mother with a lump of fish perched like a big pimple on the end of her nose. She was beautiful, even when grappling with gefilte fish.

The food was for Pesach. The first night was always spent with Mama's family and Martusia knew that people who had nowhere to go for the Seder – that wonderful Pesach meal – would eat with them on the second night. Being a widow with a small income from her millinery shop never stopped Mama from being kind and generous. There were many lonely Jews in Zloczow, and they became part of a big family for one night of the year.

Mama started early in the day, mincing fish with boiled eggs and onions, then mixing them in a huge bowl with raw eggs, crumbled matzah and what seemed like an enormous amount of salt and snowy pepper that always made them sneeze. Martusia was allowed to mix it all with her hands before rolling enough oval fish balls to feed a very large number of people. Then the balls were boiled in fish stock which was seasoned to be sweet, yet salty at the same time. Her last job was to decorate each boiled fish ball with a piece of cooked carrot before everything got cold and the jelly had set on the fish.

Later in the day Mama always insisted that they take some food to the local orphanage. It's what they did before every major Jewish holiday and every birthday. That was normal.

But after the war what is normal? Is it normal to be cooking without Mama? Is it normal to live in a house full of women – Felek's Belgian cousins – where there is always a big discussion to make a collective domestic decision? And why do they stop and stare at her whenever she comes into the room? She feels worlds apart from them.

Now there is debate over seasoning the fish stock. One of the women dips a spoon into the liquid, blows on it before tasting and tries to decide whether it is ready for the fish balls.

"I don't know, it needs something," she mutters in Yiddish as she slurps from the spoon.

"Salt," calls another. "You never put enough salt!"

The first turns, "Nu, so what do you know about anything! You want it to have no taste?"

Martusia listens silently, bemused by the fuss. She remembers how it was always so calm and quiet in Mama's kitchen, often with just the maid helping. They were such good cooks.

Kind, kind Dusia worked for Mama from the time Martusia was a baby. Dusia, who spent patient hours with Martusia as an infant while Mama made and sold hats to fussy customers; Dusia who rolled pastry destined for pierogi and let the child play with the scraps and taste the potato filling; Dusia who in 1940 flung herself in front of a small boy and challenged a gun-toting hooligan to kill her but leave this defenseless child alone. She suffered for this and Mama nursed her maid back to health, after which the maid declared her gratitude – often. Until Dusia eventually got married, left the embattled city and went to the mountains. Soon after, Mama, alone in the kitchen, was led away by German soldiers – beaten, bloodied. And Martusia, despairing but obediently hiding within earshot.

Now living in Brussels, Martusia tries to close down memories of how it was in Zloczow. She tries not to think about how totally alone she felt after Mama was taken away. Those hungry desperate times. Her husband taken... lined up against a wall... shot in front of her...

The discussion in the kitchen is in Yiddish, much of which escapes Martusia who only knows a few words, but she can guess what it's all about. She waits for a pause, then volunteers in French. "The way my mother made gefilte fish, she–" The startled looks make her pause.

A moment later she starts again. "She used to make it sweeter, and a bit salty, like everyone in Galicia. Maybe you make it the way it was cooked in Warsaw, with more salt. That's how Felek had it at home."

Silence.

One of the women moves towards Martusia, eyes pricked with tears.

Martusia is puzzled. What has she said?

"I'm so sorry," she sobs, "do you know how wrong we were? I am so ashamed." She flings her arms around Martusia's neck.

"For what?"

"We were sure that our cousin Felek had married a *shikse*. He has no other family to worry about him anymore. When he came to Brussels with a blonde blue-eyed wife who spoke such educated Polish, we were sure you couldn't be Jewish. Not you, so of course not your baby Helena. We were so sad for him. I am so sorry."

The women abandon their cooking and crowd around Martusia, hugging her and smearing their wet tears on her cheeks.

"How could we know? Look at you, with your aristocratic nose and your Polish style."

"That's what saved me."

"And you don't speak Yiddish. We will teach you to speak Yiddish," she insists. "You will no longer be outside the family."

Martusia submits to their embraces. It's better to have this family than none at all. She will learn to speak their way and to cook their way. What else can she do?

4

STAINS

Melbourne 1953

"I'm bored," I tell my mother when she brings me my lunch. This is the fourth day I'm confined to my bed, not allowed to play with my baby sister. Nobody, but nobody, spends as much time at home with an ordinary cold. Mum has no idea how the girls at school tease me about it.

Apart from reading and sleeping there isn't much to do, as established by the army of nose pickings lined up on the wall by my pillow.

"Helena, how could you," Mum says, screwing up her face. "Pfe! That is so dirty. You must clean it up straight away."

I dutifully wipe the wall with the damp cloth she just happens to have with her. She always seems to have a damp cloth with her – for my face, my hands, the door handles and now the wall.

"Please can I have Blackie. I want him on my bed so he can keep me warm."

Mum usually bans the cat from the bedroom but she relents this time. "So long as he is not climbing inside the bed. You don't want his germs to make you worse."

Germs?! I say nothing and the cat makes a gutter between my feet, spirals his body around himself, turning several times before falling asleep in the hollow.

What I want to do next is to draw a picture of Blackie, so Mum brings me paper and a pencil and instructs me to put a book under the paper in case the pencil marks the blanket. That keeps me occupied for quite some time. The family of cats are tiny skinny creatures that are fun to draw and scuttle off the page. Then I lie facing the wall, curled up mimicking Blackie, and I carry on drawing – on the wall.

I make the tails longer and longer, until one curls right over all the cats. Oops! I spit on my finger – I need to wipe them off before Mum comes back. Panic sets in when indelible pencil marks turn into dark purple smudges getting worse and worse the more I rub.

I steel myself for the inevitable tirade that follows my misdemeanors and Mum delivers – like clockwork. She sure knows how to shout, just like I know how to turn on the tears and apologize.

After dinner, in bed of course, Dad comes and sits with me. "You know," he says, "I think we should be leaving the wall this way, to be reminding you of what you have done. That's what my parents did when I have been fighting with my younger brother in Warsaw where we lived. I remember I have been sitting on top of a big wardrobe doing my homework. It was the only place where I can be away from my younger brothers. And when one brother did want to come up to be with me, I was throwing the ink bottle at him. It broke and a terrible mess it was making on one wall. My parents never that wall repainted and it has been accusing me the whole time we were children. It has been so embarrassing when I have been older.

"And now I will tell you the worst thing. When I was going back to Warsaw after the war, I was going to the street where we have been living when I was a boy. The street – it was bombed and there was only one wall standing where our house was being. And do you know which wall it has been? The wall with the ink, there for the whole world to see! Never have I forgotten it. All that was left of our family home has been that one wall... and all that has been left of the family has been me."

It's the first time I hear about my father's life in Poland and I want to know more, but I know not to ask. That night I dream about bombs falling and ink raining down on me. What do bombs look like, I ask my mother the next day.

Oops! Another thing not to talk about.

"Felush, how could you," Mum storms at Dad in Polish at dinnertime. I can hear them from my bedroom even if I can't really understand everything they are saying. But I can guess. "Are you crazy? Do you want to give nightmares and headaches to a seven-year-old? It's not enough that you suffer from them?"

When my parents shout at each other it's always in Polish – the language they use when they don't want me to understand. Ha, little do they know how much I've learned. They usually speak to me in French in the hope that I'll remember my first language that we spoke in Belgium. I always reply in English, to practice, I say.

Dad often peppers his sentences in English with German and Russian words as well as Polish and French, which is hilarious. And he can read Yiddish fluently – it was the language he spoke at home when he was a boy, but he never speaks it now.

Sometimes I wish my parents would be quiet in front of our Australian neighbors who only speak English. But usually, I just laugh at Mum and Dad's scrambled verbs. Mum's English actually isn't too bad, considering it's her seventh language.

Learning languages is something Mum does easily and she often brags about it. It was in Belgium she learned Yiddish from Dad's relatives, once they got over thinking she was a *shikse*. When the women thought Dad had married someone who wasn't Jewish, they told Mum to come into the house through the back door – the entrance for staff and workers, rather than the front door. I can't even imagine how insulting that must have felt.

It's really important to improve our English, Mum reckons. In those early days, as a "new Australian" (which she was forever, as was Dad), she had found it really hard to explain herself in English when she had needed it most.

Like the time when a neighbor tries to ask her something while pointing to the front yard. When she has no idea what he is talking about, in exasperation he says, "Say yes or no." Not knowing what he wants she says "No", which makes him really annoyed. She eventually realizes that all he wants to do is to run the wire from the power pole slightly across our front yard, at which point she agrees, after which they become friends.

She tells another story, over and over, of that terrible summer when I was five. Late one blisteringly hot afternoon Mum looks out the kitchen window and sees the rusty saucepan with the remains of my soapy bubble-blowing sitting on the concrete steps to the laundry. She asks me to bring the saucepan inside but I continue to swing on the canvas chair in front of it.

"Soon Maman," I promise.

"And stop swinging so hard on that chair because it will tip over," says my mother, in French.

"It's all right, Maman, I'm just swinging a little bit," I reply as I crash backwards. I cut the back of my head on the edge of the saucepan before landing on the concrete edge. There is a lot of blood staining the step and the two of us make so much noise that the next-door neighbor comes over to see what has happened. He looks at the spilled saucepan and the blood on the step as Mum tries to explain.

Luckily, he has a car so he picks me up, wrapped in towels, and drives us to the hospital, where he explains what has happened, as best he can understand from what Mum has said, The doctor stitches my head.

"Don't worry, Maman," I say in French to appease her. "I'm all right. I've been punished for disobeying you. You said you suffered a lot. It was my turn to suffer."

"Shush my darling." Mum looks startled.

Later she pours salt and ammonia, then cold water on the bloody step and scrubs it for ages. Eventually the offending stain fades, but it is a relief to her when the sunroom floor is built over the steps and she doesn't have to look at "that" place. I don't know why Mum is so weird about blood. She says it reminds her too much about Poland and I bet it's one of those things I'm not allowed to question. I don't even try.

A few years later, on a Sunday morning Evie and I are rolling around on the carpet, play fighting.

"It will finish badly," Mum warns us, but as usual we don't take any notice.

Suddenly my little sister screeches, "What's that blood on the carpet, Helen? Ooh, and your pajamas too!"

I can't understand Mum's frightened face.

"I told you not to use a safety pin," she says.

"Safety pin, what on earth are you talking about," I reply innocently. "It's all right, Evinki (I stress every syllable), I'm not bleeding to death. You haven't hurt me. Ask Mum." I laugh as I retreat to the bathroom.

Auckland 1980

"What is it with you and blood?" I ask my mother on one of her frequent visits to see me and my three daughters in Auckland. Her granddaughter's scraped knee releases a bit of blood onto the carpet and Mum blanches. It's as though she's been wounded, not Nikki (Nicolette at birth, but people rarely called her that). My youngest takes just a few moments of having her wound cleaned and a moment of being comforted, giving Mum and me the biggest of hugs, before she rushes back out to play with the older children.

Mum and I are sitting inside, hands cupping our lemon tea, just like I remember from childhood. We are eating cheesecake made to her recipe and she is approving of my efforts. The doors are wide open to the wooden deck designed to face north to capture the sun and overlook the native bush. For a few moments we sit quietly watching the children.

I welcome the native bush that creeps over the edge of the very unmanicured lawn. In my eyes it's uncontrived. Mum's not so sure – to her it looks a bit messy. But this native bush right in the suburbs is one of the things I've learned to love about Auckland. I admit there's the occasional unwelcome possum but it seems more afraid of us than we are of it.

Except for Dad who, on one of his visits, looked terrified when a possum crashed through the rangehood over the stove and dropped into the kitchen. The two of us were sitting alone, chatting quietly. I was feeding Natalia and Mum was in another room playing with Melina. The arrival of the possum was totally unexpected, as was Dad's reaction. Without wasting a moment, "Oy, no," he said as he scooped Natalia off my lap and raced out of the room, shutting the door firmly behind him. At the time I wasn't sure, but with hindsight I think he had his priorities right – saving my baby was paramount. All the same, I couldn't help laughing as I went to find a broom to shoo the possum out the back door. It seemed relatively harmless.

My gardening is fairly limited. It's just not something that I have spent much time doing. At best I might plant a few bulbs by the house and hope they survive my benign neglect. Or I might prune the grapevine. Reluctant gardening is one of those things that sets me apart – a misfit in the Auckland suburbs, just like the misfit I was at school when I couldn't speak English like an Australian.

Not gardening goes hand in hand with not wanting to boil fruit to pour into glass jars during the heat of summer. I could never see the point, but that just proves that I'm not a normal Kiwi housewife, despite being explicitly told what is expected. It seems that bottling fruit is an obligation for many of the women I know. In the heat of summer, they go through the ritual of driving slightly north to the orchards to buy boxes of ripe fruit that won't last any longer than a couple of days. Then they have to get to work sterilizing jars, washing, peeling, slicing and gently cooking the fruit in sugar syrup before bottling and sealing. Everything else has to take second place until each jar is carefully wiped and labelled, and the benches scrubbed to prevent an ant march. I really don't understand it.

Truth is, I probably wouldn't have been a normal Australian

housewife either. For me and my group of friends whose parents were from Europe and grew up in Melbourne there were different expectations. Our obligations were to get an education and a proper career (just in case we need it), but more importantly, marry a good provider and produce a new generation to replace the many lost lives.

I'm most comfortable knitting, knotting, stitching, drawing or pottering in the kitchen with my barefoot princesses, teaching them to make the exotic delicacies I learned as a child. I eventually do explore the Edmonds cookbook (a New Zealand cookery "bible") after receiving it as a gift from a well-meaning acquaintance. It's certainly different from my food-stained *The Complete American-Jewish Cookbook* and my well-thumbed Robert Carrier tomes.

I know that teaching my girls to cook has been the right thing to do when, with little assistance, they start to make pikelets and scones like real New Zealanders – better than I can. I am amazed at how Nikki at the age of about three confidently climbs onto a stool and peels carrots (and occasionally a thumb). Cute, and so competent so young – always hard-working and eager to please. Natalia turns out to be a perfectionist in the kitchen while Melina reads out recipes, organizes and delegates. I love how the kitchen is always full of laughs.

"Nu, so what is it with you and blood," I repeat.

"Oy darling, I am remembering Poland."

"What about Poland?"

We've finally reached the stage when Holocaust stories are in the public domain a whole lot more, and Mum is occasionally willing to talk about the past.

"The blood on the carpet reminds me of my mother's blood on the carpet in the apartment in Zloczow. The Germans must have been rough with her before they took her away, and I couldn't help her.

"For years I have tried to forget that pain. And to forget the frightening scenes of people who suffered beatings and torture and shootings in the street, and for what? How can there be a reason? The streets were filled with blood some days, and smelling even more horrible when the sun came out. I was always hating the smell of blood after that. That's why I have used extra perfume every month. Ach, blood stains, memories – they just don't go away. Even after so many years. Even on the other side of the world."

5

EIGHTEEN FOR LIFE, TEN TO REMEMBER

Melbourne 1956

"*L'chaim*," cheered my parents, raising their glasses. "To life," boomed my father. He always said it loudly, as if to prove that he was alive. And free.

I wasn't sure what my school friend might be thinking as she listened to my family chanting blessings over candles, wine and bread. I had never tried to explain about being Jewish to Judith, and she had never asked. I cringed in anticipation, wondering what my father would say next. This might be the first and last time I invited anyone to stay. What if Judith's parents were Baptists and didn't let her drink wine?

I knew a bit about Baptists. "The Baptist school was the only one that would take a French-speaking child," my slightly shame-faced mother had explained to friends. When we first arrived in Melbourne, Mum had taken me to a Catholic kindergarten for a few weeks. There I taught the nuns how to pronounce French words while they taught me my first words of English. Before long I was walking around the house chanting, "Jesus loves me, this I know, for the Bible tells me so." Mum laughed. She liked the fact that after two years in Belgium I had acquired a charming French accent. Whereas I could have done without the accent and without the French.

When I started going to school Mum would cut thick slices of rye bread for my sandwiches. They were so unlike anyone else's lunch that I was too embarrassed to eat them in front of the other girls. So I was always starving when I got home. And there were my un-eaten sandwiches in my schoolbag. One day Mum came to the school fence and watched me, and the other girls, to see what everyone else was eating.

That afternoon she asked her next-door neighbor about what to buy.

"White bread from the milk bar, love. And don't cut it too thick."

Mum dutifully made white bread sandwiches as instructed, then told me to bring home anything that I didn't eat. The next day I brought home my soggy sandwiches filled with thickly spread butter and sliced strawberries that had been sprinkled liberally with sugar. It took another enquiry of the neighbor before I was given an acceptable sandwich of butter and Vegemite that wouldn't be noticed.

I was seven when Dad bought Mum her first car. We loved the freedom that little Morris Minor gave us. Mum would pile the bassinet onto the back seat to take us for drives to places like the Dandenongs, and I would sit beside the bassinet to watch that my baby sister didn't try to climb out. It was so much better than getting around by bus, when the journeys with Mum always seemed unbearably long. She would insist on speaking to me in French, which was awful because everyone always looked at us. Then I'd get stomach aches whenever she tried to speak in English and people stared even more.

"Push me, pull me, but *please* don't talk to me! People keep looking," I would beg as we walked home.

And now Judith was giggling, probably at Dad's funny English and clumsy manners. He just wasn't like other fathers. I wondered what she would tell the girls at school. I decided that giggling with her was the easiest thing to do.

Dad didn't have a clue, I reckoned, about my friends – and there might be none after tonight. Nor about speaking English without Polish or Russian words thrown in for embellishment, and certainly not about doing anything remotely helpful at home. Not like the next-door neighbor or the one over the road – they were always doing jobs at the insistence of their wives. Mum joked that Dad didn't know one end of a hammer from the other, and he didn't even try.

All the same, she was loyal, even when she was furious with Dad. She reminded Evie and me in her imperfect English that he was kind and gentle and a good provider. We should all be grateful. Not everyone's father had opened a clothing factory providing jobs for other immigrants. We arrived with very little and had no home, no English and not much money. And look what a good life we had now.

I didn't mention that the neighbors gossiped about us as they stood chatting in the street, and how they laughed uproariously about our bright red kitchen ceiling. Or that the snot-nosed children in the street and at school taunted me with, "Frenchie, Frenchie," and being peculiar, because I didn't speak English like them.

When I was about five, I was sent to an old woman (well, she seemed old), who lived around the corner. She gave me English lessons. Mrs. Brown had lived in India for many years so I ended up speaking "Raj" English – beautiful English, with beautiful vowels, according to Mum – so now I was "stuck up"! It was so unfair! How could Mrs. Brown not realize that **no one** spoke like that in Australia!

Mum and I played endless games of Scrabble to improve our vocabulary. One day she triumphantly put down "vind" on a triple word score.

"What's that?" I asked suspiciously, dictionary at the ready.

"You know, 'vind,' like 'vindscreen viper'," my mother said in all seriousness. She never lived that one down.

There were times when Mum really was the living end. I wanted to die the day she charged into the headmistress's office. It had started when Mum asked politely at the beginning of the year if I could be excused from the Scripture class, but it wasn't allowed. All right, she said, I just had to learn about Christianity. There was nothing wrong with having knowledge, so long as I went to Hebrew School as well.

It wasn't too bad. I remembered the stories easily and enjoyed singing hymns. I just went quiet on bits like, 'for Jesus' sake'. The homework was easy and I did really well in the exams at the end of each year.

In my last week of primary school, my teacher asked me to stay back after class. I had topped the class but wouldn't get the Scripture Prize because they couldn't give it to a Jewish girl. "You don't go to church," the teacher explained. It seemed stupid to me but I pretended I didn't care.

I wished Mum had calmed down overnight, but she wasn't going to put up with such injustice. This wasn't why they came to the other end of the world.

"How is such a thing happening to people who have suffered such a terrible war!" she exploded to the headmistress. Loads of people outside the office heard her.

"How can you be behaving like the Germans and discriminating against an innocent child! First you are insisting she is attending your Scripture classes and she is doing the examinations, and then you are pretending she is not being top in the class!"

The upshot was that the Scripture Prize was awarded to me at Speech Night, as well as the English Prize and one for being dux of the junior school. Mum beamed with pride and I tried to forget her excruciatingly embarrassing behavior. Later she berated Dad – in English – for not coming to see the wonderful moment when I received more prizes than anyone.

"Can you believe that seven years before she is speaking only French?"

Dad hugged me and told me how proud he was, then picked up his newspaper. I had barely left the room when an argument erupted, in Polish, as always. I stood quietly outside the closed door, straining to understand the gist of it.

"Felek, for goodness' sake, you are so unfair! Even if Speech Night is boring, why can't you enjoy our beautiful, clever girls? I was so proud. Why couldn't you come just once?"

"Listen Tushinka, for one moment of being proud I should go to such a thing? You know, I promised myself a lot of things when I was in that stinking camp if, please God, I could ever get out. I had a lot of time to think about what mattered in life while I picked out gold teeth from all those dead bodies, when I shoveled bodies to be burnt and did all that unbearable work with a gun at my head."

What was he saying? The bits I understood made no sense.

"Never, never ever did I promise myself to listen to songs about loving Jesus. I don't want to be told that he is goodness when so many terrible things happened because we didn't believe he was more than just a man. That's not what I escaped for! Leave me alone. And get the girls out of that school!"

In 18 months, I thought later as I lay in bed, I can sit the exam for the best girls' high school. That would solve the problem.

"I won't mind changing schools for MacRobertson Girls' High School," I told Mum the next day, "especially if I'm not the only Jewish girl in the class anymore."

She agreed.

For some reason, the number 18 rang in my ears for days. It was like a magical number, and I wrote it over and over again, as numbers and as words, then I tipped the numerals upside down and flipped each of them back to front.

Eighteen months... What was it Dad said about the number? That's right. Eighteen was the number that symbolized life; it was made out of the Hebrew letters, *chet* and *yud* which represent eight and ten. Side by side the letters would make the word "life", and adding them also made 18.

I loved numbers and so did Dad. He could add columns of numbers really fast. I would hear him mumble in Polish as he rode up and down the columns. It was easier in his native tongue, he explained.

"Did you like numbers before the war?" I asked one day.

He usually frowned whenever anyone mentioned the war, but this time he seemed to skate over it. "Yes," he said, "but I did have to leave the Yeshiva which was my school. When I was 15, I had to be learning making shoes so I could be earning some money to help to feed my younger brothers and sisters. Later I was learning book-keeping. Now I am thinking I am liking to study about numbers and philosophy. Maybe one day."

The thought of my father as an elderly student amused me. He would have to improve his grammar and his logic, I told him. His logic was really strange and he always seemed to change the subject. I sometimes thought we were talking about something really straightforward. Suddenly he would dart off on a tangent, never to return to the main track.

If I tried to stop him, he would say, "Heleninka, Heleninka, never mind. This is interesting. Don't be angry. This is like Talmudic discussion. Not everyone is using Greek logic in a straight line." He would smile benignly, his eyes full of love, but it took many years before I understood and accepted his reasoning.

"You know darling, there are good numbers and bad numbers," Dad remarked one day.

"How can a number be bad?" I asked, scrunching his newspaper as I perched beside him on the arm of the couch.

He hugged me tightly. "You should know that a number tattoo like my friend has on his arm is very bad. All numbers on people's arms were for the Germans to identify and count their victims. They always counted people in the lines, and pushed with their guns, one into this line to do crazy heavy work, the next into another line to be taken away to be killed. Always they counted, and the numbers needed to be right, or they would beat us. You needed to have some *mazel*, some really good luck, to stay alive. You needed to be in the right line. And you know, the number six million still makes me shiver."

I shivered too.

Without stopping to think I asked, "Why haven't you got a number Dad?"

For what seemed like ages I could hear the fridge rumbling in the kitchen.

"Darling, I'm not sure you are old enough to know," he said finally. "But I can tell you this: the place where I was working has been such a place where we were getting extra food and clean clothes every day. It was not a normal camp and we were not doing normal things. So we didn't get numbers like Jews in another camp. Now finish, end of story for today," and he patted me on my bottom to shoo me away.

One evening Dad came home, tired as usual, and said he had to go out again after dinner. "Lydia's mother died and it's already two days, so after the funeral yesterday they will need me to make sure there is a tenth person for the *minyan*, to have a little service in her memory."

"Why?" I asked.

"Because we are needing ten men for some prayers – ten adult Jews – and we are needing to remember the dead. Not just at the funeral. But always. Never forget, darling, the dead are living in our memories. Ten is important for a *minyan* and saying *Kaddish*, and ten is important, like in the Ten Commandments."

I tried to understand. "Are you reminding yourself about the dead when you and Mum light those short fat candles?"

He nodded.

"But you don't pray very often. Why now?"

"For Lydia and Fred. To remember her mother who has been a good woman. She treated you like you were her own grandchild, and she lived through the worst time possible, may she rest in peace. Now Lydia and Fred have only their son and no one living who is from Poland. Like us. And they need me to make sure they have a number ten."

Dad picked up his *yarmulke*, the skullcap he wore when we lit Friday night candles. He gently kissed us goodnight. I guessed this would be a night of nightmares and headaches.

I never told Judith about Dad's nightmares and headaches. I didn't think she would understand. She must have thought we were a pretty weird family, though she never mentioned it. We never talked about things that really mattered, but she wasn't mean to me like lots of the other girls, and it was nice to have a friend. The two of us worked on our geography project and played Monopoly and cards all weekend.

What a pair of misfits we are, I thought on Monday morning as we waited quietly at the bus stop, both of us with glasses fogging up, gray raincoats flapping around our legs. We weren't like the others who pulled their tunics up at lunchtime, so their legs would get sunburnt – that was against the rules. We were more likely to sit in the shade playing jacks. And I wondered whether Judith's parents had things they never talked about to her.

6

TALKING FUNNY

Melbourne 1957

"Mummy, why do you talk funny?" Evie asks. My little sister has arrived home at the end of an afternoon of playing in the street, the embattled but conquering heroine.

Mum sighs when she sees her six-year-old's appearance, her dark blonde curls and clothes spattered with mud, but she gets more worried when I get into a fight. We've all learned that Evie can look after herself; she is so much like other children born in this country. On the other hand, I am referred to as her delicate European flower – give me a break! But I do like reading books, preferring to avoid rough play.

I'm sitting on the edge of the bathtub, grinning as I watch Mum fill it and helps my sister peel off her filthy clothes. Evie is covered with damp bruises, shining like trophies.

"What you are fighting about?" Mum asks. "You know that never fixes something."

"Johnny said that you talk funny and that we're weird. I told him he was dumb, so he hosed me, then I threw mud and stones at him, so Pete and Andy joined in... Three boys against one girl! It's not fair but I showed them, and they cried and I didn't." She finally draws breath and pokes a cheeky face at me.

"But you really do talk funny, and 'specially Daddy."

"Listen darling. Talking differently is just part of who we are and where we are coming from. We seem weird for some people, but we are not so boring like them."

"Yeah. They're just jealous we got a TV and they haven't got one. Anyway, they'll never come over now."

"Evinka, listen to me. I am telling you again and again, a good person is not fighting. And maybe one day you will be speaking more languages too. Then you will know you are not sounding always like everyone else in his first language. So long you can be understood, it's not so bad. Can you imagine if these boys must speak Polish or French?"

Evie giggles as she splashes in the bath, and Mum gets that far-away look. I wonder what she's thinking. Could it be about other times, other languages? I know she speaks heaps of languages and she's talked about not always fitting in. Not that Evie's old enough to understand. I reckon there must have been times during the war when speaking like other people must have been really important. But I'm not going to ask her about it – I don't want to set her off.

The next day I rush into the house. "Mu-um! Mu-um! Where are you? Quickly! Evie's killing Johnny and his Dad is coming over. Says it's the second time this week and he won't stand for it. Quickly Mum!"

Mum comes to the door to say hello to the neighbor, wiping her hands on her apron. He is swearing loudly as he strides towards the front door with Evie trailing behind him. He has been gardening and his gumboots leave a muddy lumpy trail on our clean path that Mum has just swept.

"Good afternoon, Mike. How you are? Is there a matter?" she asks sweetly.

"You could bring up this ratbag daughter better, that's the matter! Bloody little... She's a menace," he says shaking a finger at Evie. "I don't want her near me boys!"

"They were shooting me with bows and arrows."

"Really Mike. A six-year-old girl is able to upset your boys? It is possible maybe they are saying or doing something they shouldn't?

Maybe you should be asking them what they are doing with weapons like bows and arrows. They are your children after all."

"Geez Martha. You really are a bloody foreigner! You don' bloody unnerstand!"

"No Mike, in my home is nobody saying 'bloody' please. And what is it I am not understanding? How maybe I must tell Evie she must never fight boys, no matter what it is they are saying or doing? Okay, and you maybe are telling your boys how they never should be attacking girls or making funny of them and their families. We are agreeing?"

"Bloody hell! Bloody foreigners! Whoops, sorry. I didn't mean bloody. But you're all the bl… same! And it's bl … it's true, you do talk real funny!"

He leaves and Mum picks up her broom and starts to sweep the path again, quietly saying something about remembering times when talking differently caused big trouble. I suppose that's why I have to go to elocution lessons.

The edge of Lvov 1943

On advice, Martusia took refuge in a relatively new housing estate on the outskirts of Lvov. Aniela Bochensky owned the house and her son Roman and his wife Janina lived with her. They made Martusia welcome, even though her presence was a potential danger to them all, and they showed her the basement where she should hide if danger was imminent. Martusia called Janina "Aunty", even though Janina was only two years older than her. Roman had been an organ builder before the war and now worked as a carpenter. He wasn't in the army as he had lost the sight of an eye during childhood.

One day, a group of Hungarian soldiers arrived, asking for billets in every house. That was when Martusia started to worry. The men were part of the German army and the last thing she wanted was to be at close quarters with an inquisitive stranger. All the same, it was a relief that she could present her recently validated identification papers.

Imre, a courteous, educated and good-looking young officer from Budapest, moved into Janina's house. He was multilingual and spoke elegant German with Grandma Aniela, Russian with Janina and tested his impeccable French with Martusia – to which she responded curtly in Polish. His attentiveness made her anxious and she was sure he would soon realize that she didn't fit in. Many people of her age had moved to the anonymity of the center of town to get work or had joined the Polish army. Mainly elderly people and just a few parents bringing up young children like Janina were left in the housing estate. Remaining inconspicuous was difficult, however much Martusia dressed as the neighbors did.

Imre reported that the other officers were envious of him living in Janina's house. In the past Martusia would have loved male company, to relax and flirt, but now she just wished they wouldn't visit so often, or pay her so much attention. When Imre tried to draw her into conversation, he would ask why she never stayed to talk with them, but she remained monosyllabic and withdrew to the kitchen or the basement, which was really out of character but seemed safest.

One balmy evening Janina and Martusia were sitting by the window to catch some air. They were knitting garments from old unraveled sweaters – a very modest source of income. Janina's husband Roman sat smoking a cigarette. Their young children, who called Martusia "Aunty Marta", were with Aniela. Smoke filled the air, wrapping around all of them like a shroud before escaping out the window.

Outside it was exceptionally quiet. Inside, apart from the clicking of knitting needles, all that could be heard was Roman, wheezing and sighing. Then they heard it – a rhythmic k'chunk, k'chunk of boots moving towards them. Martusia became more aware of the smoke filling the room and struggled to breathe calmly. Her knitting needles slipped to the floor. And they all waited.

... deafening marching footsteps... should they be hiding... what is it that she fears?

After what seemed like forever, the marching stopped just outside their window. There was muffled talk, followed by a long silence. Then a terrifying screech...

The noise modulated...

A tiny string sound.

Followed by a long pause...

Suddenly a sonorous Hungarian gypsy melody and singing filled the air. Martusia's heart beat wildly for a long time afterwards. How dare those men frighten them like that! All the same, the music was a welcome diversion.

The following Sunday she and Janina were invited to accompany the soldiers to church. The offer had been made week after week and Janina repeatedly made excuses. It was not the "done" thing to be seen promenading with people from a foreign army, she explained, even if they were living under the same roof.

"You should come dancing with me". It was a request rather than a command.

The atmosphere was calmer since the evening of serenading and Martusia allowed herself a smile as she shook her head.

"Please, you can't keep refusing me."

But she was too cautious to even thinking about enjoying herself, so she continued to keep her distance.

... dancing... whirling in and out of the arms of her beloved who drew her to him... she felt his lips caress the top of her head... it was all she dared remember of her husband...

After the soldiers had been in the village for a couple of months, Janina was asked if she would mind if the men had a party at her home. A small gathering. She couldn't think of a reason to object.

Martusia announced that she would be out that evening. There was nowhere for her to go, so she spent several long uncomfortable hours wedged into a dark cupboard in the basement, dodging the attention of a large rat. Its eyes were pinpricks of light that stared at her between bouts of fruitless searches for food. She felt lucky it didn't try to eat her.

"Believe me, I would have much preferred to be with you," she apologized to Imre with heartfelt sincerity next day when he told her how offended he was. But there was no menace in his tone.

One evening, not long after the party, Imre came in very drunk. From his pocket, he pulled out a photograph of his mother and began to weep. Loose threads hung on his uniform where once there were epaulets and insignia. It was as if he'd been in a fight.

"What happened?" Janina asked.

"The Germans have ordered us to go," he sobbed. "We must leave tomorrow morning. All of us except our doctor must go. The ambulance will go later. Martusia, I would give anything for you to come... Be with me, be our nurse or something. I have asked the doctor to bring you if anything goes wrong here. I asked him to save you, no matter what."

"You what?!"

This was the last thing she wanted to hear. It was one thing not to be convinced by her false identity papers, but to suggest to the Hungarian doctor that she was in danger? Worse was to come. The doctor in his naivety told his landlady, who immediately confronted Janina.

"Listen, I know Martusia's not your niece. Look at her – she's not like us! She's Jewish! You need to get rid of her before everyone finds out. We could all be killed."

The company left, leaving Martusia panic-stricken, which was compounded by the arrival of a new group of Hungarians needing billets. Now there was no way she could go anywhere without drawing attention to herself.

A Hungarian officer introduced himself to Janina in faltering German, announcing that he would move in. He asked if they spoke Hungarian and Janina muttered tersely, "Polish". While he was busy organizing the other soldiers Janina and Martusia had a hopeless discussion about where she could go.

That evening the officer sat with them, telling them in his clumsy German about his wife in Hungary. Martusia was puzzled as she looked at him and realized that not one of the soldiers who arrived that day had any medals on their uniform.

She listened to the conversation then asked boldly but quietly in German, "Excuse me, are you by chance Jewish?"

Janina's eyes indicated her terror.

"Of course not, I'm... I'm married to a Scottish woman," as if that had any relevance.

"Well, you just used the word *chaverim* which even I understand. Did you mean *kameraden,* the German word meaning friends. Who taught you this Yiddish word?"

He put his head in his hands. Finally, he said in a low voice, "My grandfather was Jewish."

"And do the Germans know?"

"What can I tell you? Probably. When the Germans invaded Hungary, they knew there were Jews in the Hungarian army. Everyone in our company, maybe even the doctor, is related to a Jew. Hitler now demands that every one of us, no matter how distant our Jewish connection, must have our epaulets removed, stars taken off... every sign that we are officers. Now we are to be plain frontline soldiers fighting for the Germans. That is the way he'll kill us!

"At first the Germans said this was to trick the Russians, so they wouldn't know that we are officers. But I know that's not true. We have been stripped of rank, degraded... we will be the first to go. First in line, first to die... There is no question, we will die, maybe even before we fight."

Suddenly, Martusia understood Imre's drunken behavior on his last night with them. Maybe he had just discovered his fate, which she could only imagine. Much later she heard whispers about men being butchered on their first day of battle with the Russians... Jewish soldiers in the Hungarian army fighting with the Germans, dying on the other side of the fence. They, too, had become part of this monumental tragedy.

"You are facing a terrible situation and I am so sorry to hear it," Martusia told the officer. "But you know, that doctor who was everyone's friend, and I know he is your friend too, was so terribly indiscreet. He said things he shouldn't have. Now I have to leave and hide somewhere else, but I have nowhere to go, no money, no one who will care. So, you see I'm in a terrible predicament."

"Please, please take my wedding ring and tartan scarf my wife has sent. Maybe you can sell them for food, whatever you need... Where I am going..." He pauses, looking at the floor, "there is no need... for such..."

Next day Janina and Martusia went by tram to the center of Lvov to see the director of the library. Janina begged him to help her niece. As a result, for several nights Martusia stayed in the library ready to go wherever this kind man would send her. But she knew she couldn't stay there for long as so many people needed his help.

Early one evening he sent her to an elderly woman who kept a snarling German shepherd for company. The woman demanded payment immediately and Martusia handed her some small coins. They shared a double bed, the dog sandwiched between them. All night Martusia lay there, eyes wide open, still as a corpse. In the morning the dog accompanied her to a filthy toilet and growled as it blocked the entrance.

"Lice-ridden mongrel," she muttered, scratching herself.

The old woman heard her. "You'd better get out. Fast," she said, "You speak Polish like a lady, but a Polish lady would never stay here. I know you're Jewish, even if you don't look or sound like it. You can have this bread and cheese but I'm not taking any more risks. You've had one night. That's it!"

The director of the library was frantic when Martusia returned.

"Listen, I can't keep you here. You were lucky you weren't here last night. The plain clothes Gestapo came back early this morning before I arrived and took everyone who was hiding in the library. Go back to Janina. Please!"

She walked away slowly, imagining what happened. She had heard about it all before... she knew what kept happening.

Queues of trembling people... all desperately muttering prayers to a God who seemed not to listen... wetting themselves in fear, their hands raised...

made to walk interminable distances... forced onto trucks, trains... taken who knew where... to be shot... like her mother... like her husband...

She was too anxious to go straight back to Janina so she just kept walking around Lvov, wondering where to find food and shelter, worrying about what would happen next, and wishing that maybe, maybe one day there would be much smaller things to worry about.

7

THE BEST

Melbourne 1961

"What for you are fighting with your mother?" Dad asks, lowering his newspaper. "You know she is right, even when she is wrong. For so many years I am telling you that you should listen to her. She is the best mother in the world."

I stare at him in disbelief. I don't for one moment think that other 16-year-old girls have to put up with this rubbish. I raise my eyebrows in the direction of my younger sister before exploding. "You have to be kidding. Do you really believe what you just said? Boy, has she got you wrapped around her little finger."

"Helen, stop!"

"Well, I'm not going to be painted and displayed like a trophy, and paraded in front of pimply boys and women dripping in gold jewelry with nothing better to do than to criticize everyone's dresses! I don't want to spend half a day at the hairdresser! Or hours at the dressmaker! I don't want to be like that! You can keep your curtseying and the self-important creep you curtsey to and those stupid frilly white dresses! Debutantes are ridiculous!"

"Helen, please. Don't be like that. You are not having to do it. You know that we–"

"–just want the best for you," Evie and I chorus.

"Oh Da-ad! I wish you wouldn't go on and on about the best mother and the best children in the world. It's suffocating. It's always, 'We don't want you to suffer like we did'. Well, you never tell me how you suffered, so how am I supposed to know what on earth you are talking about?"

The moment I say it I know I have gone too far. Dad's face turns to thunder and I see the pain in his eyes. Damn, now I'll be blamed for his migraines and sleepless nights. It's not that I mean to hurt him. He's not that bad really. He only ever smacked me once when I was five and I was being a real brat. But he is so pathetic about Mum, and she always has to be the perfect mother. They try so hard!

I go to my room.

I don't know much about their wartime experiences. "Don't ask," Mum would say with a theatrical sigh, "it was too horrible to talk about. We lost everybody. We are lucky we are making a new life in a new country."

"I don't want to boost," (does he mean boast?). "I don't want that you are thinking I am a hero," Dad said, his voice trembling, "It was survival."

And another time... "People are doing terrible things when they are being desperate". I try to ask him what he means but he prefers to talk cryptically about black times in the past and lighting up his life now.

"Is that why you keep all the lights on?" I ask thinking about how often he says, "Heleninka darling, put me on the light."

"I lived in darkness for too many days after being in the Death Brigade," he explains.

"The Death Brigade?" I know I'm on dangerous territory, but he did say it, and I really want to know.

"A stinking hellhole! One day maybe I will tell you," Dad says quietly, his eyes glistening in a way that reminds me not to ask any more.

"Only 13 of us survived," he says unexpectedly one Sunday morning.

I stop buttering my toast, too scared to ask a question that might stop him talking.

"Do you want not to know?" he asks, his dark eyes looking sober.

Tears sting my eyes. "I can never do the right thing," I say, trying not to raise my voice. "If I ask you, you put your newspaper up between us and fall asleep, and Mum blames me for your nightmares. And now you want me to ask? Well, I don't want it on my conscience that I was the cause of your migraines or your heart attack. If you don't want to tell me, then don't, and I'll never ask, and I'll never know. But it's not fair to play these games with me."

After a while Evie comes to my room.

"Dad cried," she says.

"Don't tell me! I suppose Mum talked about his migraines and nightmares, which I know he gets. And if we dare to say anything to her, she feels sick and faint, which makes me feel guilty. And he tells us that we shouldn't upset her because she's our mother, and she's perfect, even if she isn't. And who cares if we're upset? I know they're right, but it's so unreasonable to expect us to know what to say."

"The war stuff does it." Evie is bright for a ten-year old, even if she's a tease and a pain most of the time.

"Yeah, well we'll never understand, especially if they don't tell us anything."

"I heard them talking in Polish. They still think we don't understand, but I get some of it." Evie grins.

"Dad talks about how he can't understand people telling their children war stories which will frighten them and scar them for life. Doesn't he know what we learned at Hebrew School?"

"Yeah. The Sunday School..."

"...that's actually after school on a Tuesday." Evie's good at making me laugh.

"And Mum said that she would go to her grave with secrets in her heart. What do you think those secrets are, Helen? What do you think happened? And what's with Dad's stuff about, 'I don't want you to think I'm a hero'? Can you work out what he's talking about?"

"Nup." I'm not quite truthful.

Evie still seems a bit young to talk to about what I know about the war – far too young if Mum and Dad are not even telling me.

"Come on Helen. What do they say in Polish when they don't want us to understand?"

"They're so obvious, aren't they? I wish I knew more Polish but I sometimes get the hang of what they are saying. Actually, it's often pretty boring."

Evie refuses to be sidetracked so easily.

"You're as bad as Dad when he goes off on tangents. Come on, I want to know about the war. How did they survive? Tell me! Go on! All they say is that no one else in their families saw the end of the war. They're keeping secrets for sure."

"Yep. I once heard someone say something about Dad breaking out of a camp."

"Did they have camps like camping in tents?"

"No, like the most awful unimaginable prisons. It's pretty amazing to think he really did that."

"You're kidding! But Dad's not like that. He's even pathetic about hitting flies. And I don't believe we are so pathetic that we should give in to not knowing. I wonder what it would take to get him to talk."

"Don't even think about it! Please Evie! Promise me. Or you'll start World War III. I know because Mum yelled and yelled and yelled at me when I tried to get him to tell me stuff."

"Okay, I promise. For now. But what if we never find out? It's so unfair! I want to know!"

I shrug, thinking about scraps I've picked up over the years. I've been told not to ask so many times that I've held back. But it doesn't stop me from listening to adults talk, from trying to picture Dad breaking out of a camp. I wonder what he had to do. Anything I imagine seems totally improbable for Dad, a man who turns away from the sight of blood. ("Please to cook my steak well done. Extra well done.") Whatever happened, it had to be something really bad if he really wants to forget.

Sometimes in the shower, I try to imagine what it was like for those poor people standing under a shower of poison gas. Water pours over me as I stare up at the nozzle agonizing about those naked people – men, women and children – about to die. As my tears wash away, I wonder how women managed in the camps when they had their periods. Did they still have them? And I sometimes lie awake at night, listening for guards and dogs. How blinkered are Mum and Dad not to realize how much I know! Not to mention how often I think about the stories I've heard.

I remember when I was very young and Dad would call Mum – "Tushinka, come to the table and sit with us", and Mum would reply, "For goodness' sake, Felush, there isn't a maid here like we had before the war. Who do you think will bring food to the table?"

Was Dad trying to normalize his and Mum's lives? Whatever they said and did, there was always at least a tiny reminder that they had had a life before the war. A war they had lived through. And survived. The exchange was repeated over the years as they adjusted to living as far away from Europe as possible where Dad learned to pick up his empty plate to put in the sink.

The conversation at dinnertime is subdued. We're about to tuck into a moist lemony cheesecake Mum has baked. It's her specialty, although sometimes she puts so much cream into it that it's on the verge of collapse. Like today.

Cheesecake always makes me think about the Sundays when Mum and Dad would take us to a cluster of Jewish cake shops in Acland Street, not far from Luna Park. Evie and I would invariably try our luck, asking to go on the rides, but we were never allowed.

Instead, we would stop at Scheherazade for a drink – a hot chocolate for us and coffee for them. Or maybe a lunch of wiener schnitzel with boiled potatoes and sauerkraut. Mum would sometimes have borscht with yoghurt or boiled potatoes. Or our favorite at any time of day – *blintzes*, the delicious sweet pancake packages fried in butter, the creamy cottage cheese and sultana filling oozing onto the plate.

Mum makes delicious blintzes and when leftover cottage cheese goes almost moldy, she rescues the remains and makes her famous cheese spread. She melts a knob of butter in a saucepan, throws in the cottage cheese and stirs until it is almost liquid, at which point she hurriedly whisks an egg and pours it into the saucepan, along with salt, paprika and caraway seeds, and stirs quickly. Onto a wet flat plate goes the cooked mixture which is covered with greaseproof paper. It sets in the refrigerator and she presents it as a gourmet spread for bread. I really like it. It's nearly as good as Dad's favorites – the smelly cheeses that are kept in the laundry so as not to contaminate all the other food. Mum doesn't like any smells and talks about how her mother didn't either, to the point of fainting when a customer who smelled dirty came into her shop.

Everyone at Scheherazade, well, all the grown-ups, seem to know each other and speak loudly in Polish. Mum and Dad always look so happy to be with them. Evie and I usually sit at a small table by ourselves and whisper a running commentary on some of the ridiculous things people are saying. They are such gossips, and have no idea that we can understand some of what they are saying.

Once when Evie got bored, she put her head on the table, and Mum quickly said, "Evinka what are you doing?" Always quick to be cute, Evie pointed to a sign for Everest Icecream. "See, it says 'Eve rest', so I am." "Evinka, not at the table, not here, what will they think?" There is often a, "What will they think?" which irritates both of us. Who are the anonymous "they"?

Eventually we wander down the street with Mum to buy a cheesecake just like the one she makes. The best cakes come from Monarch, with its fantastic window display of beautifully decorated little works of art, none of which Mum would ever buy. Ach, much too sweet! While she shops, Evie and I stand in the street staring through the large front window, trying to guess which cakes are filled with cream – which we both love – and which ones have marzipan that, we decided a long time ago, just sits on our tongues, feeling like sandpaper. Ugh!

Later in the day, when guests arrive for afternoon tea, I hear what sounds like Mum passing off the bought cake as homemade. I can never understand why she needs to pretend when everyone knows you can buy them. Evie and I don't agree about much, but we agree about cake, and we think it's ridiculous to pretend like this. Especially when Mum's cakes are so scrumptious. Her plum cake is absolutely the best in the world, not to mention her babka with chocolate streaking through the middle. Why does she have to say these things? It's not war time any more when she had to pretend just to stay alive.

There's a lot I don't understand about things Mum says. Like I've been told I shouldn't gossip. Unlike her who is always gossiping. There are the times she would say, "Of this you will never speak again." It makes me a bit scared of saying the wrong thing and upsetting her. I end up only half remembering a story or hiding the identity of anyone I am being critical about. I don't always remember stuff from the past. It's like a kind of amnesia. Maybe I've parked the information in a separate part of my brain.

Mum's home-made cheesecake on the dinner table has sagged spectacularly, a bit like the mood at the table. "Why are parents so secretive?" I ask out of the blue.

The quiet before the storm? Evie's eyes widen. Not again, she signals. I can tell she's almost ready to forgo her favorite dessert and excuse herself from the table. She's an expert at starting to slip away, muttering, "Please may I leave the table," while keeping one finger on the table until Mum agrees.

"Did you know," I plough on, "that some of your friends who have daughters my age don't always tell them what being Jewish means. All those European people, your friends, they are all Jewish, aren't they?"

"Of course," says Mum.

"Well, one day a girl asked me what the silver *Magen David* was on my bracelet. How come parents don't always tell their children about being Jewish? How come they're keeping it a secret from their children? Do you think that maybe all the girls – you know the ones I mean – do they know they're Jewish now that they're older? I mean, do they have to go out with just Jewish boys like I do?"

Mum and Dad are looking at each other in their secret code way. "Listen darling, we all reacted differently after the war. Every parent does the best they can, and sometimes telling all the truth is so hard.

Your father didn't want any more to be Orthodox after the war. If I was not insisting then you wouldn't even go to Hebrew School."

"How come?"

Dad frowns before answering. "Heleninka, listen please. Who can believe in a God that lets little children like my sister's little child be killed so cruelly? Who can be believing in a God that has taken away all the nicest, gentlest people in the world? You can be believing because you are not living through that war. You should be believing.

"On the other hand, I am saying *Kaddish,* praying for the dead, in memory of so many people. I am thinking I know why, but mainly I am feeling I must. I can't explain it. But believing? Darling, that's not so easy. Maybe you will be understanding when you are grown up."

For once I'm silenced. I think of services in the synagogue, standing beside Dad. He likes the Liberal synagogue. Boys and men never sat with women in his Orthodox synagogue when he was growing up. And I like the fact that he knows all the prayers, even if it makes me cringe ever so slightly when he's so much louder and faster than the rabbi. Kaddish in memory of the dead is like a race, with Dad winning every time.

"*V'imru, amen,*" he finishes triumphantly ahead of everyone else.

It's like the way he eats dinner. Huge mouthfuls, at great speed. Does he eat so fast so nobody can snatch life away from him?

"I'm not going to be a debutante," I announce. "I'm sorry Mum. I bet the debutante thing was someone else's idea and you loved it, but they're not my family, so it doesn't matter as much as you say. And fancy telling you that I would never get a boyfriend if I didn't play tennis or lose my puppy fat immediately! Coming out as a debutante is pretty dumb when I have already been out with boys. It's a bit archaic and snobbish."

"Don't call your mother snobbish," Dad warns.

"You can't live your life through me," I continue, looking directly at my mother. "I don't have to do all the things you think you missed out on. I need to live my life my way. I'm your daughter, not your possession."

I know that the last bit really hurts. I hear Mum reminding me, over and over, "After the war, all I had was you, this small bundle of life. My only possession."

For once there's no angry response, just sad, reproachful pools of tears and a quiet, "I don't feel well."

I feel terrible and can't help thinking that Evie never has to put up with so much pressure.

Years later Evie tells me off. "You didn't train Mum and Dad very well." At 14 she has started going out with boys and is reacting to the rules. Unlike me: I had had to wait patiently until I was nearly 16.

I laugh an adult laugh. "You don't know what I started with. They aren't so protective with you. You've got it easy."

"Why do they do it?" she groans.

"Because we just want the best for you," we chorus, and fall back on the bed laughing.

8

COURAGE

Auckland 1984

As soon as Mum arrives, my girls rush to hug her. She's come to stay for two weeks, to be here for Melina's birthday.

"Safta, Safta!"

"Come and kiss me, my darlings. Look at you all – Melina, and Natalia, and Nikki. I can't believe how grown you all are. Just wait and we will look inside my suitcases. I hope the clothes are big enough."

Mum comes when she can, and my daughters all adore seeing her. I'm sure it's not because she always arrives with a case full just for them. Over the years, it's meant toys, games and expensive matching outfits. She would reason that you can't buy such luxuries in New Zealand, and besides, it gives her so much pleasure.

I love watching how the sisterly squabbles subside when Mum spends time with them. She's such a loving grandmother – something I've never had. In fact, I've never had any close relatives. I'm not even sure I know how to relate to a big family. It's something I talk about with other children of survivors.

There are some distant family members – cousins Mum and Dad each found after the war. Travel was a big part of their lives and they visit family and old friends whenever they can. I have yet to meet all of them.

Mum found her cousin Sophie Schorr (who married Julius Reiner and lived in the US).

There are a few cousins on Dad's side:

Bernard Weingrod, who survived Treblinka, and his wife Sarah, living in Paris. Later their sons Jose and Michel and their families would become friends of the next generations.

Fanny and Marc Baumgarten and their family in Brussels, and Fanny's aunt in Antwerp.

Helen (née Weingrod) and Izzie Levine live in New York. Their daughter Karen and her husband Alan Gelb have become the nearest and dearest cousins to Eve and me.

Felka Freitag and her sisters in Israel (on the Ash side). Felka's son Gideon Markham (previously Mahonbaum), came to live and study in Melbourne in 1962. He and his family will later become the owners of the iconic Monarch Cakes.

I believe there was family in Rhodesia whom I have never met.

Before she leaves Melbourne, Mum always checks whether I can now buy the things that were missing from the shelves when I first arrived in Auckland in the 60s, like long-grain rice and aluminum foil. Those conversations now seem ridiculous.

As I recall, I never really cared that much about the sort of rice you could or couldn't buy. None of us have ever gone hungry. Not like Mum and Dad did.

Mum and I used to laugh about the differences between the two cities. She would tell me stories about arriving in Melbourne from the sophistication of Europe and remembers her dismay at how drab the city was, and how many things were unavailable.

But she would never mention how war-ravaged many of those European cities were, preferring to talk about the glamour of Paris and the unspoiled elegance of Prague. Like Crakow where I was born, Prague hadn't been bombed, so all the beautiful buildings had remained intact.

I moved into a modest house a while after my marriage ended. It was chosen to meet my needs and those of my girls, with a bedroom each. The first time Mum visited me here she declared: "Darling, it's a 'two-thirds' house, haha, and the garden is like a jungle that will bring rats if you aren't careful. You should be grateful there are no snakes in New Zealand or they will be hiding under so many weeds."

As always, her comments made me feel a bit defensive, then a bit guilty, knowing she might be right. Her chatter was often overlaid with something I couldn't quite put my finger on, something no one else could deliver quite like she did. As soon as she stepped inside, she would cast her eyes around my slightly muddly, 25-year-old architect-designed house, superficially tidied in honor of her visit. At first, she wouldn't say a lot. She just looked. Was she looking critically? Why was I worried?

I have fond memories of our first home in Melbourne with its compact rooms, intimate like this house, and so unlike the spacious luxury of Mum and Dad's more recent homes. I'm comfortable here; it's a place where I don't rattle around when the girls are with their father or friends. Importantly it's my home, in my style, pictures on the warm white walls, the nooks and crannies filled with things I love.

More than once, on the way to the airport at the end of her visits, Mum has suggested that she pay for some household help, maybe a gardener. Each time I reply with righteous indignation that I will employ someone when I'm earning enough. We're fine, I promise, and to be honest, the girls would just make a mess as soon as the place is cleaned. But thank you.

Sometime after we have moved in, Mum comes to visit and, as always, checks the house while I look on a trifle anxiously. She steps into the small garden with its new planting and smiles approvingly at the native ferns and spiky cabbage trees that randomly push their way to the light, attempting to reach above the magnificent canopy of pohutukawa trees. The plants share the ground with large healthy weeds. I wait for heavy breathing, but Mum is quiet for a bit. Maybe I've been defensive too many times.

"Come, Helen, I want to show you something I brought for you. Isn't it beautiful?"

The enameled copper picture, my mother's latest artistic effort, is cheerful as always, with more than a passing stylistic nod to Chagall. I wonder what I can safely say to her so I give a non-committal nod of the head.

"I'm sure someone will enjoy cats and flowers on their walls," I say quietly.

She doesn't let me off the hook. "But it's for you."

"Thanks Mum, but there's no room. We haven't even got enough room for all our other things."

"Have it anyway."

I hold my breath and count to ten before mumbling that maybe the children would enjoy a new creation by their grandmother. They love her artwork. I just wish Mum wouldn't constantly thrust her art on me while challenging me with watery eyes. I know she's being generous and loving, but we still struggle with each other. Besides, I do enjoy her unusual re-assembled ceramics that seem to have a life of their own. They are amongst her best works and I'm happy to have them.

I need a diversion. "Let's go for a walk along Takapuna beach while the weather holds," I suggest. "It'll be refreshing after sitting on a plane. But we need to go now, before 'it's raining cats and mouses', as Dad says. The thought makes us both smile.

The girls scamper ahead happily, kicking up a cloud of white sand. They know the beach well and head for the rock pools while Mum and I saunter along the shore line. Streaks of gold play on the calm expanse of teal blue, which is backed by the charcoal gray cut-out that is Rangitoto Island rising against a cloud-smudged sky.

I vaguely think of taking Mum across by ferry to this dormant volcano, but then I remember how she gets seasick. And if I think about it a bit more, she would really dislike ruining her beautiful Italian shoes on the rough terrain, and complain that there was nowhere to have a coffee. I feel stupid, and guilty that I've even contemplated something so wrong for her. I'll have to save that outing for my sister, when she comes to visit – if she ever stays long enough.

Guilt has been my companion for decades, in fact since my first real memory. I was aged three when we crossed the equator aboard the Toscana on our way to Australia. Early in the day I had been disobedient and I was threatened with punishment, so I was sure it was my fault when King Neptune tried to drown Mum in the swimming pool. At least that's what I thought he was doing. I couldn't see whether Mum was laughing or crying when he kept hitting her with a pillow trying to knock her off the pole straddling the swimming pool. It took years for me to understand the playful ritual.

As an adult I experience guilt as a silky petticoat that slips and slides under my skirt, clinging to me and making me uncomfortable. I've never been good at peace-making with half-truths but I'm annoyed with myself when my candor replaces diplomacy. That look Mum gives me is so much worse than our shouting matches. Why are we so desperate for each other's approval? And how come my younger sister seems to get off so lightly – is guilt the prerogative of the first-born? Sometimes I stand outside myself, watching, as Mum and I verbally engage, clumsily, painfully, like amateur wrestlers. But we do it without an audience, when the kids are otherwise occupied. On the other hand, there was often a ready audience when I was a child.

Mum and Dad always loved having visitors, often small tightly knit family groups. As I grew older, I realized these people were filling the emotional spaces for each other, spaces that should have been filled with close relatives. I can only imagine what has happened to all their grandparents, aunts, uncles, brothers, sisters, cousins... But as a young child in the 1950s, all I could see was a roomful of smothering, opinionated people who spoke the same sort of scrambled English as my parents.

I shudder when I recall some of those Sunday afternoons. At

times I was the puppet, answerable to Mum's every whim, to be laughed at and to do as I was told, so sweetly.

After arriving in Melbourne in 1949, we lived in what was then the outer suburbs that had previously been market gardens. Home on this "other side of the world" was an ordinary little dark red double-brick house in Murrumbeena, with a primly trimmed front garden boasting sweet smelling rose and daphne bushes, and pretty flowers like pansies. They formed a frill around a lawn which was mowed to within an inch of its life by a neighbor. Certainly not by Dad, who wouldn't know how. His only impacts on the garden were the tracks he left as he drove off the edge of the concrete driveway and dug grooves in the lawn. Besides, his job was to earn the money, Mum said, and she knew that her job was to manage how to spend it.

About a year or two after we moved in, Mum was relieved to get rid of the smelly spider-filled dunny that stood in the middle of the back garden and yay, it was replaced with a proper toilet inside the house. About the same time a real refrigerator replaced the ice chest. I wasn't sorry to see the "outside toilet" go, as we euphemistically called it. When it was freezing cold in the middle of the night, Mum had this idea that I should use a potty. Like a baby. But I did miss the ice chest. It was fun to have big lumps of ice wrapped in hessian delivered twice a week, and then watch the ice melt... really slowly... drip by drip... trickling onto a tray at the bottom.

Our house was a clone of every alternate house on our side of the street. On the outside nothing much distinguished us from our neighbors. Inside it was another story. No one else had a bright red kitchen ceiling. It was like our signature. No one else had a large black piano that their Mum played, jammed in beside a surprisingly large table almost filling the dining room, with only just enough room for chairs. And no one else had brightly colored ornaments with intricate detail, bought on the Côte d'Azur when I was a baby, probably out of Dad's casino winnings. That's what Mum reckoned. Even the bookshelves attracted attention. They overflowed with hard cover books in Polish, French and even a few in English and Yiddish. Only Dad could read Yiddish, and for quite a few years he brought home weekly Yiddish newspapers.

We had a television set that showed flickering black and white news, and comedies like, "I love Lucy." Dad boasted that it was one of the first sets in the country, and he bought it in 1956 so we could watch the Olympic Games that would soon be right here in Melbourne. He thought we might even go to some events. The neighbors, who contrived to set foot in the house just to see what it looked like, invariably stared, and their children were allowed to watch TV, and would sit quietly on the floor in straight rows.

Before anyone came to visit by invitation, we tidied the house – to make a good impression. When Dad wasn't sure what he should do next, or wondered where Mum was, he would whistle to her and she would reply with the same signature tune that had been theirs for as long as I could remember. I often wished I was able to whistle like them. It must have been so comforting, to know how they could find each other in a crowd.

Sundays were visiting days, and when it was our turn to entertain, the men gathered in the sunroom my parents had added at the back of the house. The sunroom was brightest in the early morning and was where Eve and I usually played. When visitors were expected, the dress-ups and toys were tossed unceremoniously into the big drawers under the built-in spare bed.

In summer we could cool down in the sunroom where glass doors opened out to the garden to let in a breeze. There almond and peach trees blossomed, then bore fruit, giving Mum so much pleasure. She told her gardening neighbor that she had light fingers. "Green fingers," he corrected. "You don't want me to think you are a thief!" She laughed and it became a much-repeated story in her repertoire.

We had a canary that I had named Peter and he lived in the sunroom, but on fine days Mum would hang his cage on one of the fruit trees or the clothes line. She would whistle to the bird and he would whistle back, a bit like Dad whistled back to her. One day she accidentally left the cage unlatched and Peter flew away. All her whistling didn't bring him back. The neighbors were on the lookout and anyone who saw him tried to hose him with water to make his wings heavy and able to be caught. Eve was inconsolable. Then two days later Mum heard Peter whistling and she whistled back and quickly put the open cage outside. To everyone's astonishment that little yellow bird flew straight back into the cage and lived to a ripe old age. And Mum was the heroine – she loved that.

The sunroom took on another life when Mum and Dad decided to have a party, usually in late summer to coincide with Mum's birthday. She did all the planning and someone brought in a huge table to be covered with the most fantastic food Mum could make, with help from a solid-looking Czech woman called Carla. Carla bossed me around and sometimes I was cajoled into helping. My specialty was to prepare the repetitive bits, like carved radishes and cucumber spirals for decorating enough platters and bowls to feed an army, although I wasn't sure how big an army was, and Mum didn't have time to explain. I just knew that everything had to look, and taste, perfect. And there had to be lots of it.

Way before the party Mum spent weeks drawing and painting on large sheets of brown paper from Dad's factory. She then covered the boring wooden fence with these huge murals. The rotary clothes line was covered with massive crepe paper flowers and lanterns, and a wooden dance floor was brought in to cover the balding patches of grass. The radiogram was dragged from the lounge to the sunroom and everyone brought their favorite records. Sometimes Leo Rosner would play terrific music on his piano accordion. I heard Mum once say that music saved his life but she was unforthcoming with anything more than saying something about a man called Schindler.

Sometimes the party had a theme, like, "Come as a song" or "Arabian Nights", and all 50 or 60 people dressed appropriately. They seemed to love dressing up as much as I did. It was a real spectacle, and Mum's were the best parties anyone gave, if you believed the phone calls she received the next day.

When she was really young, my little sister slept at someone else's house on party nights, but I was allowed to stay and help serve drinks and food. I didn't mind as I really enjoyed watching the women whirling on the dance floor and flirting with other people's husbands, who in turn tried to kiss them. I would stand in the sunroom and try to whirl, just as they did.

On Sunday afternoons when visitors came for an ordinary visit, I loved listening to the men standing in the sunroom, loudly pontificating about business and politics. They talked over the top of each other, swearing in Polish, German, Russian, with bits of English thrown in. I laughed with them about the Australian obsession with sport, and how the whole city stopped just for a horse race.

The best thing was that the men didn't know I was listening from the kitchen – they were too absorbed in their verbal footy match. It's funny how they barely paused to down their shots of brandy and whisky. Drunkards they definitely weren't, not on Sundays or even at the parties. Not like our neighbors who would drink and drink, with visitors or alone.

The younger children usually played outside or crowded into the bedroom that I shared with Evie. There weren't many children of my age to play games with and there was no way I would go near those snotty little ones, which meant I had no excuse when my mother asked me to help serve the afternoon tea.

The small lounge, with its over-stuffed dark maroon furniture, held the heat, so it became oppressive when it was filled with perfumed women, who would sit bolt upright, with never a slouch. They were meticulous about how they dressed; a run in a stocking was a catastrophe and bright red lipstick was constantly touched up. Their equally bright red nails were shaped and polished to perfection. Mum reckoned no one could possibly imagine the lives of these women just a few years ago. They had so much courage. I had no idea what she was talking about.

Then one Sunday she spoilt everything. "Play for us, Heleninka. Play maybe 'Für Elise' darling." A royal edict would be less demanding than her laughing commands. I wanted to shrink like Alice, paint myself with invisible ink... Anything rather than this.

I gulped. "Please Mum, not now."

"Go on sweetheart, play. Or maybe recite that poem your teacher was saying you do so well. You know, 'The Cataract of... Lo... Lodore ...' you know, something like that..."

I scowled at the expectant group waiting for me to go slipping and tripping over Robert Southey's words. Nah! No way today! I loathed being paraded like a performing seal and I hit wildly at the piano keys, willing it all to end. As the women clapped, I ran to my room, relieved that the little kids were outside. As I hurled myself onto my bed and covered my ears, Mum's voice, in Polish, rose above the hubbub.

"Can you believe it? My Helena was top of her class in English after speaking only French after we lived for two years in Belgium."

I just wanted to die.

The only time I didn't have to be perfect was when I was asked to speak Polish, which I did with bad grammar and apparently a funny accent. I didn't understand much Polish, but by listening I had learned to say a few words, never expecting Mum would laugh at me like this in front of everybody.

"Heleninka, say a few words in Polish," my mother taunted one day as the women ate cake and drank black tea, lemon rafts afloat. The sugar cubes would drown and dissolve, just like I wanted to.

"You know, we never taught her Polish. We found out she just picked up a few words. It was so funny," Mum told her friends as I ran out of the room.

For a single, uncontrolled moment I hated my mother. Then I retched as a sick feeling of guilt overcame me. It seemed to go on forever.

Auckland 1984

When Mum phones to tell me she's making her most major artwork and needs my help to draw it to scale, I am happy to oblige. I had planned to come to Melbourne in a few weeks, but she wants me to come really soon. While she talks, I check my diary. It sounds urgent, so I reschedule some appointments and work late for several nights to accommodate Mum. I'm racing to get everything done before I leave, but I know better than to ignore her phone-call the next day.

"Helen darling, I want to talk to you again about this project, even before you come. This artwork is for the outside of the synagogue and will be enormous, bigger than anything I have ever made, and it's in seven different, asymmetrical panels, all covered with colored glass pieces. I wanted to ask you how will we make the small drawings bigger?"

"Mum, this project sounds incredible. Don't worry about making the drawings to scale. Draw them how you want them and we'll draw a grid over the drawings then draw a much bigger grid on your big sheets of paper. Are you getting some help with making it?".

"Oh yes darling. It's impossible for just me to make it by myself. But first I have been reading and talking a lot to the rabbi. He made many suggestions and we decided it will be called 'From Creation to Redemption', with different stories like Adam and Eve with the snake, Noah's Ark, maybe God giving the world the Ten Commandments, probably one panel about Israel, and so on. The rabbi explained why seven panels is a good idea, and that reminded me how seven is such an interesting number."

"Mum, you're full of surprises. You never told me you knew anything about all that numbers stuff."

"Oh yes," she enthuses. "I had an uncle who knew a lot about gematria. You know, like you learned at Hebrew School. When I visited him, he would talk to me about the seven days of the creation and seven days of the week. I'll tell you when you come to see me. I am so glad it's soon. I always miss you and the children. It's so good it's their holidays and at last you can bring them."

There's the guilt again. I never visit her often enough, never bring the children to see her often enough. I sometimes wonder whether living in another country is my awkward way of escaping, but would I ever admit that to Mum? Or to myself? I no longer dwell on the fact that it was a husband who brought me reluctantly to his home country. Now Auckland is my home, and my children's home, and the "suitable" professional Jewish husband and I are no longer together.

"How come we've never heard much about this uncle who knew about gematria?" I ask Mum as we settle down to talk.

Unexpectedly, it's just the two of us. My girls have gone out with

Eve, and I'm enjoying the grand apartment in East Melbourne that fills a whole floor of the building without the usual hubbub of others around. There are magnificent views over the city and each time I come to Melbourne I'm bemused by how the five-bedroom apartment has been transformed into a lavish single bedroom apartment that can only just accommodate me and my family. There is a less than comfortable fold-down double bed in Dad's study which was originally two of the bedrooms; a single bed in a small room decorated Asian-style beside the main bedroom, and another two beds get squeezed into Mum's studio.

I wander around the spacious living rooms – no wonder Mum reckons my house is pokey – and I examine the transposition of what I lovingly remember of the two-story home in East St Kilda of my teenage years. In that house I had a room of my own, unlike sharing with my little sister in our first house. Strangely, we had liked sharing a room – most of the time.

The best room in the East St Kilda house, was what Mum called the ballroom (how pretentious!). It was where I had parties and where our rock'n'rolling and stomping would shake the downstairs chandelier (which came with the house and was even more pretentious!). This was where I played table tennis with my friends, smashing the ball as hard as we could so it would reach the French doors to the balcony. It's where we mucked around, where we played the baby grand piano, did the twist, and fell onto the floor laughing as we contorted our bodies to limbo under a broomstick. It was here that my girlfriends and I danced and sang along to 'Whatever Lola wants" and "Rock around the clock" as loudly as we could.

I set up my sloping drawing board on a stand in that room while I was studying architecture, trying to make the best of my student years living at home. Living at home was a given. After all, how could Mum's only possession, as she often described me, leave home to live somewhere with friends before getting married! And then when I actually did leave, she was heart-broken that marriage took me so far away to another country.

The drawing equipment was something I enjoyed using for many years. I would hitch a wooden T-square to a cord that ran down the side of the drawing board and I would balance an adjustable set square on it. Sheets of Letraset were spread out on a small desk, and pieces of butter paper with my sketches would fly around the room whenever I opened the French doors. A cracked pottery mug – one Mum had made – held the clutch pencils and pens I still use. And always in sight, was one of my treasures – a beautiful geometry set of compasses and dividers that was a gift from Mum and Dad's close friend Fred Stern, who had been an engineer before the war and had survived with his wife Lydia in Siberia. Engineering was a career he couldn't continue in Melbourne so he became production manager in Dad's factory.

Today I've decided to be totally positive about Mum's drawings. She pulls out sheets and sheets of brown paper and black and white sketches. Then she sits hunched on the couch, frowning before straightening up. I sense she's trying to find her way into one of her rare stories of the past, and I so hope she won't censor it.

"Listen darling, I want to tell you about that uncle who knew gematria. My uncle was a clever, tall, good-looking man."

I try not to laugh. All Mum's stories begin with men who are tall, good-looking and well educated. Otherwise, she isn't remotely interested. Men have to be a good catch, and heaven forbid they should smell of sweat. Pfe! I wait with uncharacteristic patience and pour a cup of tea for each of us.

"You remember how I told you that my father died of dysentery when I was a baby?"

I nod, thinking about the grandparents I've never known. There's a faded photo which I love looking at. It's the only photo Mum has of my grandfather – an earnest young man in his army uniform. Someone gave it to her in 1946 and she treasures it. Whenever I see it, I feel so sad that she grew up never knowing her father. That must have been so hard for her.

"My Mamushka was very much in love with my father. She vowed that she would never allow another man into her life while she had a daughter to bring up. Someone once told me that she would send all the men away, telling them to come back when I was grown up. It drove the matchmakers crazy. But she believed that it wasn't safe to have a man in the house with a daughter who, if I say it myself, was quite pretty. I remember especially when I was maybe twelve years old how one man courted my Mama, who was petite and had so much style. He was such a nice man. I couldn't understand why all of a sudden, he didn't come to visit any more.

"Anyway," she continues, looking somber, "during my school holidays I sometimes went to visit that wealthy uncle I was telling you about."

Mum's arms tighten across her body as she talks. I know better than to interrupt. One wrong word and she's likely to clam up and throw a loud sigh of exasperation in my direction.

"At the beginning of the school holidays, my mother would take me to the nearby place where my uncle lived and he would bring me back home at the end of the holiday. Mama was so happy that he was taking so much interest in me, that he showered me with presents. He would tell her how much he loved me and how he was happy to give me anything I needed."

For a few minutes there's silence, and Mum stares at the expansive view – is she imagining Poland in the hazy distance?

"But you know something? I didn't want to go. I hated, hated, hated it! I didn't want to stay there and I made an excuse every time Mama arranged it. She couldn't understand why, and it took a long time before even I realized something was wrong. We didn't talk about things like you do. I'm not even sure why I am talking about it now."

Mum pauses again, squeezing her eyes shut and sucking in her breath loudly, releasing it even more loudly, over and over.

"You know, for all those years I never told Mamushka what he was doing."

A knot grows in my stomach during the even longer silence that follows.

"He was such an intelligent and generous man, and she needed his help with money for my education. How could I tell her that I hated him coming to my room every night... stinking of nervous perspiration... and how he would tell me I was the most beautiful girl in the world, and all the time... ugh! pfe! Making me promise that it be our secret..."

"Did he...?" I almost choke on my words, knowing the answer as I look at my sad mother. Her tears dribble into her cold tea. A hundred drums beat inside my head.

"I was lucky not to get pregnant. I was so naive I didn't even know that it was possible. It was such a different time. I envy you so much being so open. You know, I couldn't be a virgin for my first husband. Don't ask me how I got through that, explaining I had an accident from a horse! My life has always been about pretending! If you only knew how much I have had to pretend! Who can trust any man?" she explodes, and falls silent for several minutes.

"You know," she sighs, "my art is my therapy. No counsellors, shmounsellors... This way I can think about beauty and color and happy things. Not such horrible reality. The only person I ever told was my friend Lydia before she died of cancer – she should rest in peace. But not your father, not my first husband – nobody else has known. And no one else should know. It's strange that I'm telling you. But that story lies like a stone inside me for so many years. I needed to tell..."

Mum's face is "white as a sheet," as she would have described it. I'm starting to understand how come she suffers – from stress, from ulcerative colitis. What courage to have held back for so long, not saying anything. And what courage to have told me. I look at her through my tears. The memories of violation and loss of trust seem to have added wrinkles to her face just in the past hour. I hope she doesn't regret telling me.

As I move to embrace my weeping, shaking mother, a pile of sketches spills onto the floor. I'm holding her close when a piece of paper floats away from the pile. I become transfixed. Nothing of my mother's art has ever been anything like this. Vicious slashes depict barbed wire, and black smoke belches from a chimney in the background. Ghostly, naked figures with bald heads huddle in a lower corner of the page.

"What's this?" I hesitate before picking up the drawing.

"It's time. I couldn't put the war in my art until now, but I know I must, before it's too late. I need to open the gate on that nightmare, to get rid of the poison that has been making me sick. And I want to show the world what happened to my beautiful mother who never found love again, and my first husband whom I adored, and my aunts and uncles and... you know, even my uncle didn't deserve to die like an animal! Nobody deserved to be killed for nothing, or tortured, or buried before they died! I'm making this work of art so maybe... maybe later I can die in peace," she whispers.

I continue to hold her close and we both weep for some time.

It's the only time Mum talks to me about my great-uncle. I'm not even sure how much she tells Eve. She probably assumes I will tell her, which of course I do. Sometimes I wonder whether I dreamed the story, but it seems to make sense in a weird way. All that flirting, needing to please men, never trusting them, being offended by perspiration... I'm not a psychologist – that's my sister's profession – but I know enough to work out some of it.

The conversation and the sketch haunt me for months. Mum's insistence that she will create a panel to commemorate one of the most traumatic chapters in history sends shivers down my spine whenever I think about it. She's clear that she will include it alongside all the cheerfulness and optimism – the sunshine, rainbow, flowers and doves she is using to represent the Garden of Eden. What a courageous, revolutionary move in her art. And how inspirational for me in my art.

The mural is a protracted project. Suddenly it is less important.

At the beginning of August 1985 my sister phones. "Helen, you need to come over quickly. It's Dad." I manage to get on a plane to Melbourne the next day and go straight to the hospital.

"It's the fourth heart attack and it's the worst," Mum tells me tearfully. "We didn't tell you about the one he had when we were on holiday in Surfers Paradise. We didn't want to worry you." I experience a tangle of emotions and more questions but hold my tongue. I send Mum home to rest and take my turn at Dad's bedside.

"So, Dad, you kept your health a secret. I'm so grateful for the secrets I now know about your life, and hope you haven't held back too many more. Anyway, I love you so much."

My father tries to rearrange the tubes that are irritating him and smiles fondly. "Darling, you have given me the greatest gift of all – three gorgeous, healthy, intelligent granddaughters. I am so proud of you, and them.

"Heleninka, listen please. I've been thinking that you know enough stories about my life. You are right, not all, but enough. You don't need to know more. You just need to remember what you can and say *Kaddish* in memory of our family. It must be you, and Evinka, as I have no sons. No one else is left. And I love you all so much.

"The seven women in my family – you know, seven is a good number, with lots of interesting meanings. Seven: your mother, you and your girls, Evinka, and her baby girl... these are important. Your love for your parents and your children – they are the most important things. Like it says in the Torah.

"But the stories of the past – ach! You know how I have always been telling you, 'There is only one day that counts–"

"You can't undo yesterday and you have no idea what will be tomorrow," I finish.

He smiles. "Good that you remember. I don't have the will or the *koyach* for talking anymore about the past. Now please look after Tusia. Your mother has so much courage but right now she needs you more than I do."

Dad closes his eyes and I gently adjust the bedclothes and sit with him a little longer. It's my last coherent conversation with him. After this he just wakes occasionally and tries to smile. The doctor tells me Dad seems stable and if I need to, I could fly home. A day later Eve rings to say he has died. I fly back to Melbourne with my children.

There are definitely things neither Eve nor I will ever know, but

I'm grateful for the stories he has told, grateful for the kind of man he has been – humane, loving and generous. If only he knew how much courage his wife had during the years before those they shared. If only I visited my parents more often, listened to them more and criticized them less. If only I didn't feel so guilty. If only...

9

HAVING BABIES

There was a time when Mum was in hospital in Auckland. Probably the late '70s. She had fallen ill on one of her visits, so Eve flew across the Tasman as soon as I phoned her. We both knew Mum would need someone close by on the return trip and it had to be Eve as I couldn't leave my young children.

In hospital we sat by Mum, staring at the blood the nurse was extracting from her arm.

"Blood tests, blood tests," she complained hoarsely. "I have no veins left. Look how bruised I am. Maybe you should give them your blood instead." It seemed a strange thing for her to say.

The next day started early, at 5.a.m. to be precise. The phone call from the hospital was followed by frantic activity as we rushed to Mum's bedside. She was dozing restlessly when we arrived. Her breathing was heavy and she looked so pale. We sat silently stroking her hands and watching the monitor. After what seemed like an eternity, she opened her eyes and smiled. "My two beautiful babies. You know, you will always be my babies, even though you are having your own children, Helen, and please God, Eve, you will have children too. It's funny. I never realized how alike you are until now. Maybe it's the light," she croaked.

"We don't look alike Mum. We never have," Eve replies quietly.

Melbourne 1988

I step into Mum's hospital room and find Eve there, sitting on the edge of the bed, stroking Mum's papery hand.

"Hi Helen. Mum is just about to tell me what it was like when she had me."

I kiss my mother and hug my sister who carries on talking.

"Was Dad pleased to have another girl?"

"Evinka, Evinka, for goodness' sake, what do you want of me? You want I should remember so many years ago?"

"Sure."

"Actually, the strangest thing was the nurse. She came into my room saying, 'Hello Mrs. Ash. Take your teeth out love, and put them in the glass by the bed,' and she straightened the blanket and made the corners of the sheets tidy. I remember how I have been staring at the woman, thinking what for goodness' sake is she saying. I am in a hospital to take out my baby, not my teeth.

"She tried again, more loudly, and more slowly, like I am an idiot. I am sure she is saying under her breath, 'Bloody foreigners!' So many times I have been hearing people say that. But I didn't speak such good English so I was just shaking my head, and lifting my shoulders, and I was wondering if was she meaning me. The next time the nurse came in she didn't ask. She just put her hand in my mouth and pulled my front teeth. I was nearly choking and pushing the stupid woman away. I was screaming at her, 'You are being crazy? What you want with my teeth?' The nurse backed off, pretending to smooth her very tight uniform across her body that was like an egg, and she stared at me like something was very strange. 'It's okay, love. You just settle down. Are they your own?' I was perplexed too. After a minute of no talking, nothing, she burst into such loud laughter. 'You must be the only one in the ward. Don't worry, love. I'm writing a note on your file so no one else will maul you, or you might take a piece out of them.'"

Eve and I are laughing. "Mum, that's so funny, except it must have been horrible for you. It's really weird that people used to have all their teeth pulled out. Anyway, tell us more," Eve asks.

"Can you imagine how I have been feeling? I remember how all I was wanting was to be comfortable between the painful contractions, and I was not understanding what the theatrics could be about. My teeth have been the least of my worries. I have been lonely and no one was understanding me."

"I suppose no one came because Dad was sick in bed when you had Eve." I manage to get a word in.

"Yes, I have been worried about your father and who would look after his business while he was having whooping cough. Would kind Mrs. Brown who was living around the corner make proper school lunches for you, Helen? It was so good of our next-door neighbor to bring me to hospital. They have been good neighbors.

"Next time the nurse was coming back she was with my doctor and straight away he was bending down to examine me under a sheet, not saying anything to me. In the evening he came back wearing a dinner suit because he was going to an event. He checked again and announced to the nurse, 'The baby won't come until the morning'.

But that is not what happened. I was in such pain I called the nurses and screamed because I had terrible pain. And they were telling me to be quiet because I was disturbing everyone on the ward. But I knew that with such contractions and such pain my baby was coming soon. Almost at midnight it became an emergency so the doctor was called away from his fancy party and arrived exactly when you have been born. The terrible pain was finished and I have been exhausted.

"'I am so happy I am having a girl again,' I told the nurse, and kissing your soft blond hair all the time. You have been such a beautiful baby. 'She is like me this time, not like my other daughter who has dark hair, like her father.' You know, Evinka, I have loved you straight away, like I have loved Helen straight away. And then I was seeing a beautiful big vase of flowers."

"Were the flowers from Dad?" I ask.

"But wasn't he really sick?" Eve asks.

Mum is strangely quiet for a moment.

"Ach, how can I remember? Probably from a friend. What does it matter?"

"Maybe a secret admirer?" Eve can't let go.

"Evinka, I had so many friends and the whole room was filled with flowers."

For years after Dad died in 1985, Eve and I would talk about whether Mum had had a lover. Maybe more than one. Sometimes when I really thought about it, I reckoned it was definitely a possibility.

"Do you remember how strange Mum was that time we talked about the flowers she received when I was born? She always loved being the center of attention, and she was pretty quick to tell us about the many flowers she had received from so many people."

"And Eve, do you remember her flirting? Even with my boyfriends, which was excruciating. And she was always talking on the phone. There was a particular quiet telephone conversation that finished abruptly when she spotted me within earshot. She hadn't heard me come in from school and she was sitting on the floor, murmuring into the phone for more than an hour. She was speaking in English, which was unusual. Most of the time she would speak animatedly to her friends in Polish or German. Still, what did talking softly on the phone in English prove? It's not really evidence of anything, is it?"

"Except, I wonder..."

The next time we talked, Eve put forward her latest theory. "I've got this nagging feeling, you know, how you and I are so unalike in every way."

"Oh God, Eve. Not again! I was born in Poland, you were born in Australia, and there's six years between us – that made a huge difference to how we were brought up, what we ate as babies – all that stuff."

"Yeah, but I reckon there's more. Maybe we aren't really sisters. Well, full sisters."

"That's only one step better than your childhood insistence that you were an adopted orphan. Maybe you should just let it go."

Eve won't be stopped. "At first I thought you might not be their kid, maybe a war baby they found, and now I feel strongly I have a different father."

"That's stupid. This isn't a movie."

On one of Eve's many business trips to LA where she's working on another project, she includes a stopover in Auckland to see me and my girls. They adore her and she loves them – it's almost as if they were her younger sisters. She carries photos to show me my little niece and nephew whose father is taking care of them, along with Mum checking on them when she can.

'Oh Eve, you're making me clucky. I so love babies and your kids are so cute. It must be hard to be away from them for days on end."

'Yeah. I think I'll try to do more at home. Coming to Auckland is no big deal, but LA is a *schlep*."

It's one of those late summer afternoons we cherish – just the two of us, strolling along Ponsonby Road before a meal together. Luckily, it's school holidays so Eve has spent time with her nieces during the day. She comes home laughing: "Your kids are so funny. They think I lead them astray, and then call me a cool, almost old, aunt. I just love them to bits."

I've prepared some food for the girls to cook for themselves, along with instructions to please clean up afterwards and keep the music down. "That must be wishful thinking, but it's giving you a night off, which I bet you need. Besides, there's so much to talk about. In relative peace".

Ponsonby Road turns out to be a bit of a dodgem course as we avoid the pooches tugging at leashes, not to mention groups of young corporate types heading for a drink, three abreast, each with a jacket slung over a shoulder and loosened tie dancing in the slight breeze.

Eventually we reach a favorite of mine.

"So, Eve, I meant to ask you, did you know that Mum had an abortion?"

"Yeah, I think she did tell me. But it's the first time you and I are talking about it."

"I remember it was years after she had you. What made me think of it now was seeing those photos of your little darlings. I bet Mum is all over them. She adores little kids…"

"… and would be the last person to have an abortion. I'm sure Dad would have loved a son and I always wanted a little brother!"

"Well, it kind of makes me wonder about her deciding to have an abortion. Not that I wondered back when she told me. I suppose I must have been about 16 or 17, and I was hanging about on her bed watching her getting dressed to go out. We were talking about girl stuff. You know…"

"Yeah, every once in a while, she's done that. Some of her really good moments."

"It's weird that she came out with it, just like that, as though it didn't matter much. She actually blamed it on Dad, said that he wanted her to have the abortion. She might have said more but clammed up when she heard him calling her with his special whistle…"

"And she replied with the same tune. I love how they used to do that."

"Thing is, I never got around to discussing the abortion with her again. You know how it's always been, trying to find the right moment to talk with her about real stuff. It never occurred to me to question Dad. It just wasn't the sort of conversation I had with him. I bet you didn't either."

"You're right about that."

"The bit I'm surprised about is that she actually said that Dad insisted she 'spoil the baby', which is how she described it. Said he didn't think she should go through the baby years again when she had gone through so much. Didn't make much sense to me, although it was likely to have been way after she had you. You don't think…"

"Well, it would prove my point. You'd think that after losing everyone during the war they'd be only too pleased to have a big family of their own. It makes me wonder if she had an abortion because it wasn't going to be Dad's child. Did he even know she had the abortion?"

"Dunno. And of course, she wouldn't have continued a pregnancy if it wasn't Dad's, especially if she got pregnant when he was away on one of his long overseas business trips."

'So if she got pregnant and had an abortion, it's possible that years earlier, she got pregnant by someone other than Dad and then had me. Now I really want to know. Do you think we can ask her and get a straight answer?"

"Well, you know how secretive she is."

"But Helen, maybe we could find out whether you and I are really sisters. There must be some tests."

"Yeah, and then what? We go and confront our mother who has recently had great chunks cut out of her breast? 'Hi Mum, we've proved that we're only half-sisters, so tell us about it.' Come on, Eve, you know that she'll never tell us anything that might put her in a bad light."

"Yeah, she twists every story to make herself the heroine. It's stupid to think that this would be any different, but I really want to know."

"Maybe we should leave it. Dad loved you just as much as he loved me. If he believed you weren't his, don't you think he would have treated you differently? It's not as though he deliberately left you out of his will."

'Yes, he did. Haha. He left us both out in the final version of his will, although early versions make for interesting reading."

"Maybe Mum kept it from him like all those other secrets she's kept from you, me, her doctors, everyone. You know how she brags 'I will take secrets to my grave.' Any story that doesn't make her look perfect gets censored, like those photos she cuts in half if her stomach is sticking out. Or cutting certain people out of some of her photos, leaving just a mysterious arm around her."

I go back to the "real sister/half-sister" conversation.

"Be honest Eve, tell me why you need to know. What's the point?"

"Well, I totally understand that you want our little nuclear family story to stay intact. But I'm so curious. Think of it this way. I might find out about a father with blue eyes and a crazy way of looking at everything. Someone who sped through life and loved the outdoors and... I don't know. It might make me more tolerant of Dad never being there when I needed him. He just couldn't talk to me about anything real. He was always vague, talking philosophical stuff and politics."

"Hmm, I reckon he was just old-fashioned. He never wanted to talk to us about that kind of thing. On the other hand, wanting Mum to have an abortion isn't so old-fashioned – if he did want it. Can we expect him to be consistent? Uhh, I don't know what to think!

"Mind you, he never came to any of my prize-giving nights or concerts or anything like that. He just didn't participate much in our lives except on holidays."

"Yeah, then he was really lovely with us. Generally, he just let Mum get on with bringing us up – that was her job."

"And she was really good at it. I have this vision of Mum, when she stopped her Morris Minor on the way to a school concert one evening. I must have been pretty young. Anyway, she vomited in the gutter. It was awful."

"Oh my God, Helen. Do you think she might have been pregnant?!"

"Who would know? She was so sick, but she hadn't been able to convince Dad that he should take me."

"They both had some pretty crazy blind spots, didn't they? Do you think either of them had any children in their first marriages? I mean, how would we know? Do you think maybe you were from a previous marriage?"

"Mmh. I look like Dad so I reckon I'm definitely their child. And remember, there's all those photos of them with me when I was a baby. I just have a feeling that they didn't have kids before us. Something would have slipped out by now. I mean, once or twice Dad mentioned his sister's two-year-old."

"You're talking about his sister Franka's baby, aren't you? That little child who was murdered by a Nazi. That is such a horrible story that I'm surprised he's told us about it. I feel sick every time I think about what happened. I mean, how can anyone be so inhumane as to smash a baby against a wall! I look at Ben who's two, and see how trusting he is, and I can't bear to think about the tragedy of all those children being killed during the war."

“Stop it, Eve! That’s why they never ever wanted to talk about that stuff. It’s just too painful. I’m going to do what they did and change the subject.”

It’s really unusual for Eve to be in town for longer than a night, but next day is so beautifully sunny that I grab the moment, and decide to postpone my work.

“Let me take you to one of my favorite beaches on the west coast. It’s really rugged and the kids love it. It’s a bit of a drive but it’s worth it. You can’t buy anything out there so let’s take a picnic and make a day of it.”

Eve is amused as we drive west. “And here was I so sure you were super urban. It’s really strange. This is something I never knew about you Helen. A love affair with a beach in the middle of nowhere. What next?”

“A love affair with a man,” comes a voice from the back seat of the car.

“What would you know, Miss Smarty Pants?” Eve retorts as we all burst into fits of laughter.

The turnoff from Scenic Drive always comes as a surprise with its minimal sign and sharp turn. As we descend to Karekare, glimpses of the indigo ocean puncture the myriad greens that arch over the road.

“Woah my big sister, I never thought you would drive so confidently down a winding road like this. Boy, this country sure has changed you.”

“The road was unsealed when I first came down here.”

“An outdoors adventurer! Haha.”

“Well, don’t forget you’re remembering how I was when I was still living with you at home, when I was young and naive and stupid, and you were just a kid. What did we know about anything back then? Mind you, there’s a hell of a lot I don’t know about now. I reckon my kids know heaps more than I did at their ages.”

“Did you hear what Mum just admitted?” comes from the back seat. “Young, and naive, and stupid! You heard it here first.” Raucous giggles put a stop to any meaningful conversation.

“Race you to the beach. Are you coming, Aunty Evie?”

“Yeah, soon. See you over there.”

"Suntan lotion and swimming only between the flags," I call as the girls grab towels before running off across a sun-drenched picnic area to the shady bush-clad track. We aren't far behind, and at the end of the track we watch them happily climb over the gentle mounds which tip down to a vast expanse of flat sparkling black sand. Crashing white-crested waves welcome us while warning of danger.

"This is stunning!"

"Yeah, it's a great way to shake off the cobwebs. When the tide is out you can walk for absolutely ages. I love how empty it feels. It's a great place for deep and meaningful conversations, and I've had a few down here. On the other hand, it's just the best place for doing nothing. I feel so much less burdened when I come here. Maybe a bit like you do on the ski slopes."

"Did you mention 'deep and meaningful' as an invitation to discuss my possible other father?"

"For God's sake Eve, it's possible you don't have another father. Maybe the wonderful man who brought you up is your only father. All things considered he was a good father. And I loved some of the things he said as he grappled with English. One of my favorites was when he said, 'I am springing in the air. There are kick-roaches in the shower.' So hilarious. It was in Acapulco around the beginning of 1969. We were all there with Lydia and Fred and I remember how frustrated Dad was from trying to sort out a double-booking. And we were temporarily at a hotel where the toilets didn't work, and with all of Mum's and Lydia's languages, we had no Spanish to explain the problem.

"Yeah, I don't think Dad knew how funny he was. I loved him for so much, especially the way he wanted to grab at life. Every day mattered. Do you remember those cruises he decided we needed to take. He and I never felt sick, but Mum always got so seasick, and so did you. But as soon as she felt a bit better Mum would dress up, ready to eat at the captain's table. And then there were all those fancy-dress costumes she would make – for herself, for us, anybody who asked. And while Dad went to sleep, she would party on for hours."

"Yeah, Dad was pretty special. And so was Mum. You might be right. I know I drive you mad going on about the Dad thing. All right, where are my nieces? I might risk going in."

"Enjoy, and do you mind keeping an eye on those girls while I lie here with a hat over my face?"

"Sure."

Some months later, Eve launches into one of our frequent phone calls: "I think I know who he is."

"Who?"

"My father."

"Oh no, here we go–"

"Yeah. I'm pretty sure I know who he is. Dixie!"

"Dixie? What on earth makes you say that?"

"Well, it fits with the blue eyes. I saw him yesterday at Mum's after he spent years living overseas. I hadn't seen him since we were kids. But there's a look about him that seems familiar. And remember? He was a womanizer! And we know he thought Mum was beautiful and smart because he often said so. I thought he was being sleazy, but maybe..."

"How come he was with Mum?"

"No idea. We all went out for dinner. And there was this strange familiarity about the way they spoke to each other. She was weirdly happy and friendly, but critical of his casual jacket for the fancy restaurant. He still looked pretty good for a guy probably in his sixties."

"That's so funny because when I was in Melbourne with my partner, he turned up at Mum's out of the blue and came to the theater with us. It was hilarious when Mum made him change out of his parka into one of Dad's jackets that she still had. I knew she had a special friendship with him. But your father?"

"Well, he fits the good-looking mold Mum liked. And he has a great sense of humor which she would have enjoyed. He's a surveyor, a degree Mum would have approved of. He was into boats, which

Mum wouldn't have cared about at all, but it made him totally unlike Dad. Makes him a perfect candidate."

"Eve, that's nuts! How can you concoct something like this without proof? I mean, do you really believe he's your father? What makes you think that?"

"Intuition, and it sort of fits chronologically. Mum met him after you all came to Australia in 1949 and I was born in 1951. Could be".

"You're being ridiculous. Honestly, Eve, I think you might be making up a story to fit your theory."

"Yeah, and it's crazy that we have to talk about these things on long distance calls. I wish you didn't live in New Zealand. It's so far away."

"That's what Mum keeps saying. I hate to say it, but you're becoming your mother. Or on the other hand, are you becoming your father? Hahaha. Anyway, I'm coming to see Mum in a few weeks. Let's talk more then."

I don't wait weeks before I go to see Mum – I'm in Melbourne within the week. The way she looked when Eve visited her in hospital made her ring me straight away as she is really worried about the chemotherapy and how hard it is for Mum to get through it.

Mum is so pleased to see me. "You have been depriving me of my grandchildren," she accuses me as I stand there beside Eve who is holding Ben in her arms. I struggle every time she says it.

There's no more discussion about fathers during this trip. Eve is really busy with children and work, so we barely see each other. We'll talk another time, we promise.

10

ONCE WAS A FAMILY

Melbourne 1979

We know that Dad has had a story bottled up inside him, and as long as I can remember he has been reluctant to tell it. When a friend of Eve's, Bob Weis, planned to make his film 'Proud to Live' about Holocaust survivors, including his mother Sara, he asked Eve about including our father. Knowing how Dad has unequivocally avoided talking about the war, she said she would try.

"Oy Evinka darling, I never wanted to tell anyone about it."

"I know. It's really hard."

He broaches the subject at the dinner table. "Tushinka, listen to me please darling... please. More than 35 years after... it's all come back. I can't think about anything else."

"What are you saying Felush? You want to drag it all back, not to sleep again, to have nightmares and terrible headaches like before? You want that I should watch you suffer and be helpless. I remember how tormented you were when you made that written statement for the Nuremberg trial after the war. You were so sick."

"I know, but there were so few of us left that we had to tell somebody. Yes, it was hard to do, and not just for me. My friend Kuba Kark wrote a statement. And Leon Weliczker, who became Leon Wells when he moved to America. He was so young – maybe 17 – and had written a lot down. He had the *koyach* and the courage to give his testimony in person at the Nuremberg and Eichmann trials. Then he wrote his book *The Death Brigade.* We all needed to tell the world somehow.

"And yes, you are right, Tushinka, but it's too late now. The dreams have started. Not just the dreams, but the frightening nightmares. And it's too late to stop that madman who has been getting so much publicity. Who does that David Irving think he is! He didn't see all the crazy killing and the insane coverups, the digging and the burning of bodies to hide the evidence... Not to mention the terrible suffering of the living. How dare he deny that six million Jews were killed. Not to mention the many more who were left damaged! What gives Irving the right to think he knows what was done, what was not done, to us and to our families? It certainly wasn't done to him. He can't possibly understand the pain he is causing. You know darling, I think... maybe I'm ready to break my silence. Eve is right when she says we need to tell about our lives and how we survived when so few did. It's for our great grandchildren to know. How else will they really know where they have come from? But I have to admit I'm terrified."

"Felush, listen. We came to the other side of the world to forget, to live for today and to look to the future. What about your heart condition? You know what the doctor said about avoiding stress. For goodness' sake, how will you manage to work? Oh, you are so stubborn!" She talks fast for a few minutes. Then stops. She knows him too well.

"Tushinka, you're absolutely right about everything, but I'm back there already. In my head I'm already telling the story. All night, for many nights... I'm so sorry, but I must..."

Dad's favorite place behind the newspaper offers no refuge. It's a long night of dreams of skinny dogs dressed like people in striped pajamas, all of them reaching helplessly for a field of bread scraps on the other side of an electrified fence. The bread is just out of reach. Always out of reach. Except for one small piece... Which will be the lucky one?

"It would first be a research interview on audiotape," explains

Eve. "Then if you agree, a video interview in a studio. I can go with you, and you can leave whenever you want to."

"Okay, Evinka. You are right. The world has to learn from our stories. Dragging up those memories will be difficult, and if I tell my story I don't know what it will do to me, or to you, or Helen. But I can't allow David Irving – what does a so-called academic know – to deny all that suffering."

"Thanks, Dad. You're really brave. Such a *mensch*. I'll talk to you again tomorrow."

"I don't feel like a *mensch,* darling, and now that I allow myself to think about the past it's suddenly real again. And terrifying."

I definitely didn't feel like a *mensch* when my job at the work camp was to smash the headstones at the Jewish cemetery. This was supposedly so the Germans could build a new route around Lvov for their transports and avoid the center of the city. Each blow I was forced to inflict on those stones was like they were my grandparents' graves. After all, they were somebody's grandparents.

The first job at the camp had seemed easier. My heart hurt less. We were required to carry bricks, mortar and steel from one end of the railway station to the other. At night we were allowed to return to the ghetto. But then the Germans wanted us to be more productive and to work for longer hours. It was an excuse to break up the ghetto and form a number of work brigades with us all locked in a camp.

The camp... oy yoy yoy! I have never known such viciousness, such unpleasantness and pain to so many. For what? Oy, the agony of daily beatings and shootings! We lost count of who is here today and who was here yesterday. It was a miracle that any of us lasted more than five or six months. I don't know how I stayed alive – in body at least.

We learned that to think about our families made us emotional and immediately subject to the guards' brutality. One day, I had a warm memory of my family sitting around a *Shabbos* table. I could almost smell the sweet *challah* my mother Hela used to bake. Perhaps the guard could see it in my eyes and I was beaten for insolence, luckily with nothing broken as a result. If I dared to remember that there once was a family, if I dared to frown just thinking that I would never see any of them again, I knew I would be perceived as useless, and shot. Like others, I learned to stare at my feet, freezing out all emotion. We had to block everything out. Or we died.

In my head I held an image that stays forever, however hard I tried to forget. It was the day the Germans came to Lvov and goose-stepped into our home. Franka, the elder of my two sisters, was with my mother in the kitchen and I had just arrived. The women were watching over Franka's little one, smiling at his antics, when the soldiers barged in, barking orders and demanding papers. With barely a glance at the documents they pushed the women towards the door of the apartment.

It didn't make sense to anyone. Why the women? What were they supposed to have done? Where were they being taken? Franka paused to scoop up her child but one of the Germans grabbed the two-year-old, holding him by the legs and smashed that beautiful little child against a wall. It took just one blow to kill him. My distraught father rushed forward and pleaded with the soldiers to take him and leave the women, but he was pushed aside and told to be grateful for his life. Then the hysterical women were taken away, never to be seen again, leaving us in shock, numbed.

We shed so many silent tears as we listened helplessly to more screaming women being dragged away. Nobody could believe such a terrible thing was happening. What was this brutal insanity with innocent women and children?

Somehow my wife of two years survived this. She had melted into shadows, becoming invisible at the critical moment. I held her tightly all night as we lay wide awake.

Listening... waiting...

In the morning my father Herszel, a good kind man, a religious man who loved and cherished his family above everything, moved quietly from apartment to apartment in our building to check who had been taken, to offer a prayer, and an embrace. It seemed that he needed to do something to dull his pain.

Suddenly, we heard three shots in rapid succession. We waited for him to return, too afraid to venture out. I prayed he was in someone's apartment. Eventually a neighbor came in weeping. A bullet had killed my father who happened to be crossing the courtyard at the wrong moment. It was so horrifying, so tragically sad, and we prayed that those murderers wouldn't return before the middle of the night when we took his body to the cemetery.

The next morning, we heard marching steps approaching... again. I was with my wife and my two younger brothers, and we stared at each other in desperate silence. I wished we had somewhere, anywhere to hide. This time there was no melting into shadows. Just shouting and rough handling as we were rounded up. We knew not to resist and were taken to a labor camp where we were segregated.

Later I heard that my beautiful wife Rusia was absolutely distraught when she saw the misery in the camp. Like me, she carried a little phial of what we called *svenkali* – poison that kills immediately. Each member of my family kept a phial in their underwear. Within 15 minutes of arriving at the camp my darling wife took the only route she thought possible.

My first days in the camp were a blur. I was surrounded by acts of inhumanity, sadistic torture and blind panic. There were no tranquil moments and I couldn't bring myself to pray to the God I once believed in. Yet, the beatings I received, which were for no particular reason, except I was just in the wrong place – seemed slight in comparison with the horror around me and the anguish of losing my loved ones.

One day, after about four weeks, we were marching back from working in the rain to the other end of the camp when Mikhal, my youngest brother slipped in the mud. As he started to get up, he was shot in the back of his head. I desperately wanted to rush over to him but I could see that it was too late. Besides I knew that I too would be shot if I moved a muscle in his direction. I stared straight ahead, not daring to blink in case I started to cry.

It was too much for our brother Moishe, Mikhal's soul mate and protector. Only Moishe had been able to calm the hot-headed Mikhal when they were young and in trouble, but this time he wasn't able to protect him. Somehow Moishe managed to escape into the woods nearby to join a resistance group from Lemberg, the German name for Lvov. Word reached us later about how they tried so hard to thwart the Nazis by damaging railway tracks and destroying German vehicles.

We overheard German guards talking about some Ukrainians who had helped the Jewish resistance group, and how they all worked against the Polish army. That was until the Germans offered the Ukrainians well-paid jobs. How quickly alliances can be forged and broken when people are hungry for food and power over others. These same Ukrainians who were so helpful to Moishe at first, responded to the extra money by telling the Germans about the Jews in the resistance group.

The days and weeks were agonizing, numbing, and sad news arrived in strange ways – sometimes from a bored guard, or someone outside the fence. The resistance group was liquidated, ruthlessly. All members who were found were shot.

I really didn't know why I refused to give up, even when I learned that my younger lovely sister, my beautiful, beautiful sister Eva had been raped and killed.

I was beyond tears, beyond pain, almost beyond feeling. At night, I would rummage for my phial of *svenkali* hidden in my clothes. It would have been an easy way out, but for some reason I couldn't bring myself to take it, even if I no longer felt like the optimist I once had been. I just wanted to survive one more day, one more week... I remembered the prayer that started *Ani ma amin* [I believe... in complete faith]. Maybe one day it will be better. Maybe one day the cruelty will end. I vacillated – to believe or not believe. I struggled to pray like I used to, like my father taught me, my father who had been such a good man... He had not deserved to die. None of them deserved to die...

11

GAMBLING

Feliks was always a risk-taker. In 1949, as a new immigrant in Melbourne, he rented two dingy rooms in Flinders Lane and started a *shmatte* business making men's raincoats.

While he was establishing his business he had to learn to speak English. He remembered employing a young teacher and she spent nine weeks, six hours a day, six days a week, and by the tenth week he was able to go out into the world, able to communicate in English and read *The Herald*. No mean feat for a man who knew no English before he came to Australia. He had a knack for business and before long he moved the factory to McKillop Street and added a line of swimwear for men.

"You know Heleninka, it was a lot of work, but I was believing Australia was a lucky country and if a person has some *mazel*, anyone can make a good business."

Better to be a giver than a taker, he would pontificate, and he loved sharing his good fortune. It was his way of celebrating that he was alive. After all, he had arrived with a wife and a child, and soon had a factory that produced clothes, even though he was barely able to thread a needle, let alone sew a garment. According to Mum, he started with a case of money he had brought from Europe and he borrowed a lot of money. He was quite a salesman.

Amazingly, and probably typical of the postwar economy, the business seemed to thrive from the beginning, and Dad managed to create an air of success by moving the factory to bigger premises and adding more lines of clothing to the range – for men and for women. Pride in his reputation as a businessman, and being known as a generous man, were coupled with him expounding his philosophies with friends. This was the life of comfort and flamboyant spending he had dreamed of.

He would give jobs to immigrants who, like him, arrived in Australia with very little. The story as we heard it was how these new arrivals, with little or no English, were anxious to obliterate the horrors of Europe. "Go and see Feliks" someone in the community of European Jews would say. And Dad would provide whatever work they could manage.

"Can you design, make patterns? Are you a cutter, a machinist? Can you sort and dispatch? Come I will teach you how to be a packer." He would provide anything that would give them some dignity and a pay packet. These people were forever grateful for the start he gave them, and after a short time most moved on, some to become much wealthier than Dad. Some even re-qualified in their chosen professions. Their success never concerned him – on the contrary, he was happy to have helped.

He showed the same generosity years later when I was a university student. He would tell me to bring my girlfriends to the factory for them to choose some slacks and tops which he would then give them. And he told them to come back again. Plenty of friends of my mother and sister received the same largesse.

For the first couple of years Mum was happy to help in the factory. After accompanying me to kindergarten and later to school, she would go to the factory.

"Helen, you have no idea how it was," Mum told me, more than once. "In the beginning, I was doing everything to help, chasing spiders and scrubbing the filthy little rooms that hadn't been occupied for months. Before long, I even helped to design garments. I had learned quite a lot from my mother and even a bit when I worked for the Russians in the manufacturing part of their supplies store."

Mum enjoyed telling me how she would take a train to the city. In the first couple of weeks she met a charming handsome Jewish law student who spoke German. They often traveled together.

"Did you have an affair with him?" I couldn't resist.

"Me? With him?" she protested. "Don't be ridiculous! He was a married man with a wife and children. How can you ask such a thing?" And that was the end of the conversation.

Melbourne 1984

Eve and I are used to Mum keeping secrets, and for as long as we can remember we have watched her flirt with any man she considers handsome. I really didn't like it when I was a teenager. More recently we've been less critical, but all the same we've spent hours trying to guess what went on in those early years in Australia. Mum, however, has always been reluctant to reveal anything that doesn't suit her. And talking about major health issues doesn't suit her.

"I have a lump. It's on my breast," Mum announces in one of her phone calls with me. "I've had it for two years and the new doctor says I should have it removed. He wants that I should go to the hospital."

"Two years!" I splutter into the telephone. "That's really irresponsible of your doctor. It's mad to have left it for so long! And dangerous. Oh Mum!"

'What can I say? How did I know?"

"Well, your doctor should have known."

"Oy darling. I trusted him for a long time."

"You need to get a specialist onto it – quickly."

"Darling, I don't know if I will survive going under the knife."

"Please Mum, I know it's frightening, but it's modern surgery, not how it was in Poland before the war. I know you're worried, but they do this all the time."

Mum reports the conversation tearfully to Eve. "I tried to explain to Helen I was afraid and I was hoping it would go away. My doctor friend was saying it might. You girls, you just don't understand! But the good thing is that Helen rang again to say she is coming to Melbourne as soon as she can arrange something for her children. And you know, I need to work on the mural. I must finish it after so long... Please don't be cross, Evinka."

"I just don't understand why you waited. I'm just as upset as Helen. Let's get you to hospital for that appointment, I'll cancel my meetings and take you. Mum, can't you see that it's such a gamble to leave a lump. I don't understand why you're resisting so much. Medical knowledge is so much better now. Please, please let them operate."

"That's exactly what Helen said, but I'm not sure. We'll see. Maybe. You need to understand, in Poland, going to hospital was a big, big gamble. People went there, and they died there. I don't want to die yet. You don't want me to die, do you?"

When Mum comes out of the anesthetic, she is so relieved. "You know, my darlings, I'm not really such a gambler. Not like your father was. I was just being a coward and I'm so glad that the operation is over. You'll see, if I can survive five years without more cancer, that good-looking doctor was saying that I can grow to be an old, old woman."

She smiles wanly at us. "I promise – no more gambling with lumps. The doctor was cross too. Now before he is arriving, please pass my lipstick to me."

When Dad's heart gave up in 1985, he was 73 years old. Working in his business had absorbed much of his life in Australia, and apart from the very early years, he discouraged Mum from spending time there, saying "Tushinka. What for do you need to worry about the business? Go and enjoy making your beautiful art."

Now he is dead and it's too late to ask him anything, and Mum has inherited the business.

"I could come over for a while," I suggest to Mum. "Eve and I could help you."

"What do you know about the factory! It's a *shmatte* business! It's not like what you are doing. Please stay in New Zealand. I will tell you what is happening. Maybe you can come later."

Ten days after Dad's funeral, on a miserable wet morning, Mum drives to his factory. Well, it's actually hers now, she realizes. She turns to park in Dad's spot and a car blocks her way. Slowly and carefully, she reverses out of the factory car park, but not quite carefully enough. She sighs when she sees that the paintwork has suffered yet more damage.

At the front door she loiters for a few moments and stares at the brightly colored mosaic mural outside the front door. Raindrops ricochet off the tiny glass squares she had positioned so meticulously before cementing and grouting them all those years ago. Feliks had been so proud of the mural, saying that it gleamed like a jewel. At the time she was pleased with the way the geometric slashes of sunshine encompassed the large "A". Now she isn't sure about anything.

She steps into the foyer, slowly shaking and folding her flowery umbrella, and stares at her second, much larger mural featuring two stylized armless mannequins posing against a backdrop of multi-colored fabric swatches. The mannequins appear as contrived as her smile.

"Gidday Martha," she hears as she steps into Dad's office. Nothing has changed. The family photos on the wall are still there. The expansive desk is tidy and the brightly colored ashtray with not a single cigarette butt to be seen, or smelled, is off to one side, as décor rather than function. It reminds her how she had made so many ashtrays all those years ago in her ceramics phase. How right Feliks had been in his dislike of smoking.

Mum smoked for many years. There were those happy Saturday mornings when she would smoke continuously with her friend Lydia. They would sit in the kitchen at the round table which was covered with a patterned plastic tablecloth. Sometimes a few breakfast crumbs escaped her cursory wipe when she heard Lydia arriving and they were vacuumed up by our much-loved golden labrador Rusty. Dad allowed the dog to enter the household when our cat had yet another litter and we struggled to find homes for the kittens. "Get rid of the kittens and you can have a dog," he said. We didn't wait. And Rusty ended up being Dad's most faithful walking companion.

It amused me that given how fussy Mum could be, with Lydia it didn't matter. Lively conversation, uproarious laughter, cups of tea, and loads of cigarettes would fill the morning. In my late teens, I loved sitting with them, listening to their outrageously funny conversations.

One afternoon, after coughing longer than usual, she cleared the ashtrays scattered around her studio. So many butts! So much cigarette ash falling on her pots. Pfe! No more! It was cold turkey. After a week she asked Dad whether he had noticed anything different. "A new hairdo?" he suggested. "A new dress?" She laughed, asking him how come he hadn't noticed she had given up smoking. He was so pleased. It was to be a decision forever.

"Good morning, Pat. How are you?"

"Can I help you with something, love," Pat asks Mum. He smiles at her, and all she can think of is the Cheshire cat grinning. She feels as though she is shrinking. What is she facing? Slowly, she removes her wet coat and hangs it on a hook on the back of the door. The last thing she wants is for any of the managers or staff to see how nervous she is. After all, they have known her as the confident wife of the boss. No one needs to know that all she wants to do is to curl up on the rug under the desk and have the whole problem of the factory disappear.

"I wasn't sure when you would be coming in. It seems so soon, Martha."

"Well, I need to understand what is going on here." She looks hopefully at him. "Maybe I need to look at some papers. Some accounts. A balance sheet please." She remembers how Feliks would talk about balance sheets.

"Sure," he says. "Last year's, or the draft for the current financial year?"

She pauses. Wondering. "Everything please. I need to see it all."

"Okay, I'll have them ready for you by the end of the day."

They walk around the factory and it's as if she is seeing it for the first time. She tries to take it all in – the small amount of stock, the skimpy order sheets, the machinists' schedules, the dispatch area. All she can think about it is that there are still many employees dependent on her to feed their families.

She spends much of the very long day on the factory floor, everyone offering their condolences. There are tears and hugs. Staff thought fondly of Feliks, and it is clear that he had held the business together. She talks to the cutters and machinists, the packers and cleaners – everyone, and especially to Feliks's right-hand man, Fred, the production manager who is her good friend Lydia's widower.

That night, her back aches and her feet feel like lead weights. She holds her head in her hands, her dinner gets cold, and after a while she stares at the rows of numbers that seem to leap-frog towards Springvale cemetery. "Feliks, Feliks! What have you left me?" And like every question she has asked all day, there seems no straight forward answer that she can understand.

There is one thing that she does understand. The business – her business now – has been his biggest gamble and it is no longer the busy business it had once been. She recognizes that something has to be done. But what? She feels her blood pulsing. She doesn't want his life's work to be reduced to rubble.

When she had arrived at the factory in the morning, she had started by thinking that she could take charge. In reality, she can't work out what to do. For weeks Eve puts her own business on hold and comes to the factory to help her. And to convince our mother to sell the business. Word gets out that Ash Manufacturing Company Pty Ltd will soon be on the market. All of a sudden, thanks to Feliks's accountant, she has a prospective buyer. A price is agreed. They have to do a stock take.

It's a shocking realization that the selling price has to be halved after the stock take. The good thing is that the business is sold, and later the building. Despite everything, Martha survives financially.

The whole time she was so-called "in charge" of the business, Martha has been living on valium. Her eyes are constantly filled with unshed tears, her mouth panic-dry. And she keeps asking herself, "How did it happen? What did Feliks know about the changing economy? What she does know is that Feliks had always said that he wanted to die with his shoes on.

She has no regrets when she removes the family photos from the walls of Feliks's office, just a heavy, tired feeling and much sadness. Then she turns her back on his dream, never to drive through that dingy street again. Not long after, when the buyer has not managed to turn around the fortunes of the business, the building becomes a storage facility, embellished by an out-of-character brightly colored mural. Not too many years later the building is demolished for development.

Mum's mood improved after a few weeks and eventually fewer tears fell for Dad. It's not that she didn't love him. The last few years had been reasonably contented and affectionate, but after his death there were moments when she found it hard to contain her fury. One day, Eve found her lying on the floor screaming at Dad. She was angry that he died, angry about the heart attacks he refused to talk about, angry about how he didn't tell her how he was taking such risks with his business.

Being left with a business that had kept expanding for most of the 40 years made her angriest. Why wouldn't he sell when he had a good offer years ago? She knew that going to work had been the only thing that kept him alive in the end. But really? It was bitter-sweet how he left everything to her – the damned factory, the massive loans and responsibility for so many employees, many of them Italian and Greek migrants. Oy Feliks!

It wasn't all over just because the business had been sold. There was a complex company structure to be unpicked. Even living in New Zealand I was very aware of this.

"Do you know how many people have been offering to help me? Not just Eve. Were they really trying to help me? Maybe. I don't know. I know I didn't want them circling around me."

Every time she had to deal with the accountant and the lawyer Dad had used for years she would ring Eve, despairing. "Oy Evinka. What can I do? I don't understand what has been going on."

"Maybe it's time for fresh eyes. We know Dad's affairs were really complicated. But it's okay to get a new lawyer and accountant who might be able to explain it better."

Eve rang me to tell me what was happening and we exchanged a wry laugh about Mum's infatuation with men who have degrees. She reported how old and fragile Mum looked as she wrapped her arms protectively around her belly, her eyes blinking fast. "I'm sorry," she had said quietly. "You were right. I should have let you organize a new lawyer and accountant sooner. Thank you darling."

The only good thing, Mum said when she felt calmer, was that she had won her battle with Dad to leave no mortgage on their apartment.

"Please Felush, please just one thing in my name, without loans, something separate from the factory. No more gambling with our home. I want to sleep at night!" Dad had laughed at her insecurity, but he finally agreed.

Eventually Mum resumes her work on the huge mural *From Creation to Redemption* for the outside of Temple Beth Israel that she had started before Dad died.

"You know, Helen, I have to finish it. Your father made a commitment to donate it to the synagogue. I am thinking all the time how oy yoy, your father was so quick to give, even on my behalf. He was so generous, even to anyone who would knock on the door and ask for money, he always said yes. Whatever religion, whatever charity."

"It's wonderful that you are doing the mural, Mum. Only promise me you won't drive yourself too hard. The deadline should be yours, not anyone else's."

"You are right. I don't have the *koyach* I used to, but I want to finish it, and I want it to be as good as I can make it. You will see. Will you come to Melbourne when they unveil it?"

"Of course I will. I'm so proud of you. It's an amazing project and I can't imagine anyone else doing it."

Making the mural means that for hours Mum sits in her studio that had once been a bedroom overlooking the city, in the ninth-floor apartment in East Melbourne. Whereas once she had spent time sketching the skyscrapers and spires beyond the park where she liked to walk, she is now focused on cutting glass. This has to be finished.

Mum is happiest when she works at her table, sometimes until late into the night, week after week, cutting and smashing glass shards that she glues to a base. She claims using all that force is her therapy. It's only when she looks at her manicured hands in the evening that she realizes what she has been doing. She picks out the glass splinters and watches red beads of blood fall onto the tablecloth. Pfe, blood! Always blood!

"Mum, you're amazing. Look at these panels They're fantastic!" Eve has come to check on Mum. "But you look so tired. Don't you think you should take a break? Just occasionally?"

That evening, after cutting her hand for the umpteenth time, she rings Eve. "You know Evinka, you are right. I have decided that what I want is a whole day looking at art, talking with an intelligent person, and having lunch at a nice café. I know you don't have the time so I will ring a friend now and hope she is still awake. Maybe she can come to the National Gallery with me tomorrow."

The break is absolutely what Mum needs and she returns to work on the mural with renewed energy, determined to finish the artwork. She is relieved that she is still capable of working even though her health is waning.

One evening, on a visit to Melbourne I am sitting with Mum and Eve. We gaze at the sparkling city lights and chat about the mural. It's good to see Mum making so much progress.

All of a sudden Mum says, "Your father was such a gambler."

We haven't talked much about Dad lately.

"I was always frightened he would lose everything. He gambled with that business. I think he put all his eggs in one handbag and those huge loans terrified me. It was worse than when he played poker or went to the casino in Monte Carlo."

"What was the problem with poker?" Eve queries. "Do you mean with real money? Big money? And to think he taught me to play with buttons."

"Darling, it was before you were born, when we lived in Belgium and then when we first arrived in Australia." Mum sighs.

Melbourne 1950

Smoke hovers like a cloud over the small lounge room. Martha and Feliks are visiting friends and there is just enough space around a tiny folding baize-topped table for four men to perch on stools. The men frown over their cards, muttering seriously in Polish, but the stakes are nothing compared to the risks they have taken in order to end up in Melbourne. Not that they ever talk about those times. It is enough to enjoy gambling when there is only money at risk – and needing to dodge the acerbic comments of their wives.

Feliks sits calmly, waiting to make the move that might clean the others out. He's learned to keep his eyes sober, a habit acquired the hard way in the camp. He winces as he remembers the day a guard beat him viciously just because he thought Dad had smiling eyes. Whenever he recalls that day, he can feel his aching body and sore head, and then his immense relief that nothing is broken. Not like his poor friend whose beating meant that he couldn't stand in line properly. They shot him and he died slowly, slumped across Feliks's feet.

Always more bodies in pain... begging to be put out of their misery... naked, emaciated, torn by dogs... tortured... electrocuted... hanging where they can't be ignored...

Peals of laughter distract Feliks and he hears Martha's voice. He finishes the hand in a hurry, not very well, and goes to see what is happening. Martha is sitting on his friend's knee in the crowded dining room. Instead of a cup of lemon tea at her lips she has a rose between her teeth, and is resisting having it bitten away from her. What is she doing? He turns away.

"Felek, where are you going?" she calls.

"Home. Come on, Tusia, let's go."

"Already?"

"Yes, I'm tired and it's late for the babysitter."

In the car he snaps, "I hate you behaving like that. I wish you wouldn't do it."

"And what should I do while you are gambling away the money you work so hard to earn?" she responds with equal vehemence. "You want me to sit quietly like a nun?"

They shout at each other, then abruptly stop. For a few minutes they travel in silence. Feliks stops his new Holden two streets away from home because the rough stones of the unsealed street might damage the paintwork. Martha steps out and picks her way across the lumpy terrain in her high-heeled shoes.

"Oy no," she exclaims and stoops to pick up the heel that has snapped off. She takes his arm and limps for the last few yards. "If you give up playing poker, I will stop embarrassing you like that."

He can't help himself, smiles and kisses her lightly on her forehead. "We won't talk about it anymore."

Mum pauses.

"Was that the end of it?" Eve asks.

"Sort of," she replies. "But I need to explain to you. It took a long, long time before I understood that a gambler is always a gambler. Your father never played serious poker again, but, oy, yoy, how he gambled with that business."

12

DON'T TELL ME WHAT YOU CAN'T DO

Melbourne 1955

I push aside Dad's newspaper and settle on his knee. He hugs me, smiles at my little sister who is playing happily on the floor, and tells me he feels like the luckiest person alive.

"Dad, I want to ask you something."

'What is it darling?"

"Mum says I have to do my school project on my own, but I can't do it. Plea-ease help me."

I know that Dad wants to give in. He's good like that. And I know that Mum will be furious if Dad doesn't present a united front with her. I know it's not a good idea to make Mum furious.

"Well, Heleninka, you must listen to your mother. Did you ever know her being wrong?"

"Da-ad! This is about my project! I can't do it by myself!"

"Heleninka, listen please. My father has been always saying to me, 'Don't tell me what you can't do. Tell me what you can do.' Doing your best. That is all anyone is asking."

"Da-ad, you are so... so... umph!"

I go off to my room in a huff. I can hear Dad and Eve laughing. He is probably tickling her. And then I'm sure she'll run outside, and leave him with a crumpled newspaper as usual. And memories of his father, saying, "Don't tell me what you can't do..."

What can't Dad do? I want to ask him a whole lot more but I know that Mum will be angry if I upset him. I wonder what upsets him so much, and why she gets so angry. Will he ever tell me?

Melbourne 1979

Until now I have never been able to talk about what happened during the war. It has been too difficult. But now that I have started talking to an interviewer, the story of how I survived comes rushing back...

For several nights my father Herszel's voice comes to me – questioning, explaining, even demanding, often adding a Talmudic story that captures my attention. He has always made me listen, even now, so many years after he died.

Eventually I climb out of bed and sit in the lounge room, staring at the creamy disc in the inky sky, with gray cottonwool scudding past. There are no trams, no sirens, no trucks to break the silence and I'm conscious of my heavy breathing. Suddenly Tusia appears, her face pale, and she is pulling on her pearly satin dressing gown that seems to reflect the moonlight.

"You must be cold," she says, handing me a blanket before curling up beside me, tucking her feet under the blanket. "What is it Felush? Why can't you sleep?"

For a few moments I hold the memories tightly and feel my heartbeat quicken. This happens sometimes and I have promised Tusia I will have another check-up. What will the doctor find? That I survived a war?

The more I think about the past, wondering if I have the *koyach* to talk to an interviewer again, the more I remember my father's voice. And it haunts me. "Don't tell me what you can't do. Tell me what you can do." Just like when I was a boy, and just like I told our daughters when they were young.

"So...?" I know Tusia's shiver is not from the cold.

“Maybe I will talk to the interviewer again.”

She is silent.

“I know, I know. The last thing I need is... It’s just that David Irving has been re-writing history, and his book doesn’t go away. There are people who believe him. But the world has to know what really happened, and how he has concocted such a theory that six million Jews were not murdered!”

“Felush, listen. It will be like the last time when you told the story of what happened to your family. Do you remember how you had headaches for weeks afterwards? How can you put yourself, put us, through that again! Please! It will drag out your *kishkes*, your poor intestines, then your heart will break with the pain, and then you will get sick. And then I will have to look after you until you recover. If you recover.”

She’s right, of course. She’s always right.

“Oy, what can I say? Your head is there already. Do what you have to. Do what you think is right.”

We go back to bed and I stare at the ceiling... and I remember another ceiling...

There are splashes of dark red on the ceiling, splashes that look as though they have been sprayed from a nozzle, but more likely they’ll be from someone who has been beaten to a pulp. Just more reminders that we are in a hell hole – a work camp called Janowska.

At first, Sunday is a rest day from the backbreaking work of smashing headstones – our families’ headstones – so the large chunks can be carried to another site. We try to kid ourselves that life isn’t so bad because on Sunday mornings some of us are permitted to leave the camp – with guns trained on us, and the knowledge that many of us will be killed if just one person doesn’t come back. If we have some gold coins or Russian rubles stashed away, we can mingle with the Poles and maybe buy food to add to our meager rations. For several weeks the Germans turn a blind eye to the trading.

Those rations – what a joke! In the morning we queue for a black drink resembling coffee but we all know that the liquid hasn't been within sniffing distance of coffee beans. With it comes a piece of equally dark bread, officially 35 grams, but this often seems less. At night there is some sort of soup – fairly hot, like water, with something anonymously mushy in it. It is barely enough for survival and many die from hunger.

If the Germans don't seem to care much about us getting extra food at first, they aren't so blinkered on the work site. No one escapes their cruelty, which makes "yes men" of all of us. I watch some people throw themselves against the electric fence that surrounds the camp, rather than wait to be tortured.

Death happens every day. The worst times are when the Germans get the idea that a prisoner is planning to run away. The way that poor prisoner is treated before being hung reminds us again and again that we need to be silent. One wrong word at the wrong time... It takes so little to become the next victim.

In the beginning, if anyone resists, they are finished with a shot in the head, but later the Germans decide to save their bullets and set their dogs on the offender, to maim him to such an extent that it would be impossible to survive. And they watch. And they force us to watch.

At the back of my mind is the thought that if I am truly desperate, I can swallow my little bottle of poison, which I keep hidden in my clothes. It's a possibility. Did my wife suffer less by consuming her poison straight away? Maybe that's my survival kit, knowing I could end my life, but choosing not to. Choosing... believing?

Believing isn't heroic or religious. It's inbuilt. Despite everything, I feel that maybe something might happen. Maybe somebody will see sense. Maybe somebody will free us. It's what makes me put one foot in front of the other... thinking of survival... remembering a normal life... one more day... and another day... and another... Do I dare hope? Is it crazy to hope?

One day, after we have broken stones for hours in pouring rain it's a relief to return to the barracks. But respite is short-lived when we are redirected back to the railway station to unload some bricks. Someone nicknames them "vitamin B bricks" – to give us strength.

Eventually, we return to camp to find no sign of food. Exhausted, wet and hungry, there is little to be cheerful about.

A friend calls out, "Felek, what would you like to eat now?" A kind of gallows humor sets in at times like this.

"Eat? I don't know, but I would like two black girls to cover my chest with hot sand."

"Felek, are you alright? Are you going mad?" and "What on earth are you talking about?" I hear.

"Simple. If I could have two black girls with me, I bet that would not be in Europe, and if the sand is hot, that means that it's sunny and I wouldn't be so blooming cold and wet. And if I had had the *seychel*, the sense to talk to two girls, or to even think of two girls before, I would have enjoyed today so much more."

How starved we are for light relief as well as food. Within a couple of days, 6 or 7,000 people throughout Janowska get to secretly smile about this.

Most within this group of doomed people start to develop a sense of community, a sense of belonging. Everyone in the camp, everyone in the kitchen, everyone who is hanged... it's as if each man belongs to me, like a brother. And as I did with my brothers and sisters, I silently grieve when they are taken from me.

I witness the lengths people go to for one more small piece of bread, or a cigarette, and I ask myself, who am I to judge another hungry human being? All anyone wants is not to starve to death and to be treated just a bit better. And I try to understand how someone can lose their self-respect to such an extent that they become cruel.

Take the Jewish *kapos* who police us. These men seem to lose all ability to be kind. I watch Pavel, an old acquaintance, and remember him as a gentle, somewhat anxious schoolboy. And I watch him cooperate with the Germans against the other inmates, probably believing he will be safer, get extra rations, do less work and maybe get a new pair of shoes. Who is he kidding?

At night, we have heated discussions about these *kapos*. Men who just want to survive, say some. Can you blame them? Yes, you can, says another group, when it's at the expense of fellow human beings. No one, they insist, certainly not fellow Jews, should behave viciously like they do. Many of us are bewildered by the madness and badness that captures people to such an extent that their humanity disappears, when cruelty replaces what was once maybe compassion. I struggle to forgive and wonder if they could ever regain their humanity if one day we are freed.

One night, we gather after dark and trick Pavel into entering our crowded living quarters where we seat him at one end, with everyone surrounding him, as if in a court. The light is gloomy and the air is choking. Some inmates need to be held back, like excited animals on leashes. I have been thrust unwillingly into a judicial role and I try desperately to recognize both points of view.

"So Pavel, explain to us as a fellow Jew taken from his family like all of us, why do you help the guards who are so vicious? Is a little more bread worth it? Do you no longer care about us, your fellow Jews?"

"I just want to live, like we all do. I don't want to starve to death."

"Is that enough reason to treat us so badly, so we starve to death? Have you lost all sensitivity, all feeling towards us?"

There is no answer, and the punitive response is shattering, so hard for me to take. I want to weep and feel some responsibility days later. Pavel suffers his ultimate fate when he is ambushed and thrown against the electric fence. I don't know what is worse – the viciousness of the *kapos* obeying German orders or the righteous indignation of those against them. Why do the oppressed become oppressors? What is happening to us all?

To maintain some normality, I remember the biblical teaching to first and foremost keep oneself clean. And I try to convince others to do the same, earning the nickname "Rabbi".

But cleanliness doesn't stop me from falling victim, like tens of thousands of others, to the one thing Germans and prisoners dread most – typhoid fever. Anyone who exhibits any symptoms is immediately handed over by the *kapos* to be shot and buried quickly.

For weeks I walk around like a zombie, somehow managing to keep going. Even when I am feverish and semi-conscious, I get up in the morning, sip a little drink and walk past the guards with my head held high. At the cemetery, while others work, I gratefully escape detection under a pile of jackets. My hair falls out, a bit more each day, sometimes in handfuls. There is no medicine or food to speak of.

Under cover I lie as still as I can, telling myself that I will get better, that people have recovered from typhoid fever, that I can recover too. I imagine I am eating my mother's chicken soup...

For a moment I am disorientated. Is it safe to show my head yet? It must be if I can hear someone talking, but no, I must wait until I feel the load of clothing on top of me getting lighter. I will get a signal when to get up.

"Felek, Felek!" Tusia is pulling the covers off my face. "You will suffocate under there. Come out from under the covers. What's going on? You are so still. Are you alright?"

"Oy Tushinka, I was dreaming. It was a miracle."

"What are you talking about?"

"Typhoid fever. So many people died and the miracle is that I survived. And the Germans didn't shoot me. I even joked in the camp that my mother made me out of steel. But you know, I owe it to my friends who saved my life. That was the miracle – they risked everything by helping me and I kept believing that I could survive. I know I can survive again, telling how it was in the camp. Nothing can be that bad any more. You'll see. I can do it. I will do it."

13

THE QUEUE

Auckland 1993

My outing with my mother hasn't started too well. She's come to see me and my daughters, and I really want her to enjoy the visit.

"Why you are being so impatient with me?" Mum is struggling to keep up. "I am not asking much when I am with you, just that you talk to me. Helen, are you listening to me?"

I know she's talking but it's lost on me as I fumble in my briefcase trying to locate the source of my distraction. Aha!

"Oh no! Okay. Sure. Won't be too long. I'll call you back." I sigh as I find a more accessible place for my phone. "Sorry Mum. It's work."

I turn to her and smile in apology. She looks great, as though she might be in her late-sixties, maybe early-seventies, and she still makes heads turn. Freshly blonded and coiffed, she's wearing a finely stitched black leather jacket over a peacock blue silk shirt and crisply tailored black trousers. Black Italian patent leather shoes, multiple strands of gold draped around her throat and elaborate sunglasses complete the going-out-for-coffee outfit. My adoring daughters call her a trendy grandmother, but I know it's my approval she craves. And my sister Eve's.

We walk more slowly, with Mum carefully mincing around recently watered pots of brightly colored petunias that punctuate the brick footpath. Drops of water on the pinks and purples, two of Mum's favorite colors, capture the brilliant sunshine like jewels. This is the area most like the parts of Melbourne she so enjoys. She keeps telling me how she appreciates that I've brought her here to Parnell, to look at the elegant shops, to drink coffee and eat cake. It's not at all like when she first visited me.

The sparkling colors of the flowers take me back to Mum making artworks with tiny shiny elements of color. For several years she made mosaic works – table tops featuring coins and ceramic tiles, framed pictures, and murals. I was about 15 or 16 when Mum quarantined me in my bedroom when I suffered from hepatitis. After deciding that she was the only one allowed to come anywhere near me, and no, she would not let me go to hospital, she set up a small table by the doorway and, for several weeks, after bringing me copious glasses of freshly squeezed orange juice, she worked on her mosaics. And watched me. She was a surprisingly good companion.

One of Dad's business colleagues, John Wade, used to drive from Geelong to the factory to meet with Dad, and every time he would comment on the murals Mum had created for the factory. One evening when he came to dinner, he asked Mum if she would make a mural for a cabana he was building beside his swimming pool.

She was delighted to have a commission and set about working on it, mounting glass and ceramic mosaic tiles in a multitude of colors in reverse on sheets of paper, even making tiny square clay tesserae to be assembled as a butterfly feature. I think I had just finished school for the year and I was on holidays when it was time to install the mural, so I agreed to help Mum, along with a local tiler contracted to help.

We had an early start, driving for over an hour, and all went well with fixing the tiles to the wall. Trouble hit late in the afternoon when it was time to remove the backing paper. The beautiful butterfly, which measured nearly three feet by three feet, disintegrated. I never really knew what went wrong, except the tiler was mortified and I was given a job to remove every single little tile that hadn't fallen to the ground. Mum's equanimity amazed everyone.

With the tesserae laid out on a sheet on the ground, Mum

recreated the butterfly. Then she and I, on ladders side by side, painstakingly reinstated the butterfly directly onto the wall. When the glue had firmly set, the tiler applied the grout. Later Mum and I carefully cleaned the tiles, finishing well after midnight. Our charming hosts fed us, phoned Dad to reassure him we hadn't been in a car accident and provided beds for the night.

This was the epitome of Mum's ability to improvise. It was in the same vein as in earlier years when ceramics consumed her. The broken shards that more than once emerged from her kiln after weeks of hand-forming a vase or a bowl were a potential disaster. Undaunted, Mum would re-assemble the broken pieces into an abstract lamp base. Or a piece of sculpture. Similarly, her creativity extended to making fancy dress costumes at the drop of a hat with a minimum of materials – usually on holidays. And she was happy to use me as her assistant to make a dinner table look like an artwork. It was always done with style and panache – sometimes a little extreme. But always beautiful.

In the early 70s Mum had found it hard to think of Auckland as a real city, and was amazed at how I had adapted to living in such a place. When she mentions those days, I try to shrug it off, not wanting to dwell on how I felt in the first few years when I would have liked to return to Melbourne, which I didn't do. But whenever I despaired, I would think of my parents who had had a much tougher time when they arrived in Melbourne, not to mention how they survived the war years in Poland. They had built a life out of nothing. I should at least try to cope.

Mum wants to linger by the shops. She mentions that she'd like to buy some clothes for me, but I have made it clear that I need to get back to my work soon, so to her credit, she lets that go. Eventually we reach the bank.

"I hate standing in queues, waiting, waiting. It reminds me of when I had to register my *Kennkarte*," Mum remarks.

Mention of this takes me by surprise. Mum's reluctance to talk about the past is legend, and I've been silenced more often than I care to remember.

"I'm trying to remember what a *Kennkarte* is."

'It's..." A loud noise startles her.

"It's okay, Mum. It's just a car backfiring or something. You're here with me, on the other side of the world. In Auckland." She stares blankly at me, then smiles wanly.

"I know darling... It's just... you know, it never really goes away."

Mum's eyes crumple and she sways as if in prayer. I catch her and hold her until she regains her balance. A few moments later she's flirting with the young bank teller. I roll my eyes and check my watch. "Come on Mum. There's time for coffee before we have to go. You'll like this place. It's new and they make delicious cakes, not quite like in Acland Street but pretty good. Besides, I want to know about the *Kennkarte*."

As soon as we order our coffees Mum embarks on a story I haven't heard before.

"A *Kennkarte* is a German identity card, like a passport. I had a false one during the war. How I got it, that's quite a story... maybe I will tell you sometime. But now I am remembering that choking hot day as though it was yesterday. Such a queue that day... oy, yoy, how I got my document validated was quite something. I was standing and standing for such a long time, with nothing to eat, nothing to drink. What a day it was..."

Outskirts of Lvov 1943

I am living with Janina and Roman Bochenski on the outskirts of Lvov and although they welcomed me, I am constantly aware of how suspicious others are of me. The busybodies in the housing estate would have plenty to say about me, I am sure, so I try to be as inconspicuous as possible. I spend time in the basement out of sight, or quietly helping in the kitchen, keeping quiet and doing whatever I am asked – grateful to have somewhere to stay.

Before long I am warned by a neighbor: "You know you can't stay here, not without a proper *Kennkarte* that's been stamped. Has yours been stamped? You'll get us all in big trouble if not. You must get it validated or go."

The next day Janina, whom I call Aunty, makes a small parcel of bread and cheese for us and ties a black scarf over her hair. Silently I imitate her. The sun has barely made an appearance.

Fifteen kilometers to town... tracks deepened by tanks... haunted faces, gaunt semi-naked bodies... the wounded, the old and the sick... those that could, shuffled slowly, clutching a few dusty possessions... hoping to escape somewhere, anywhere...

I keep patting my coat to make sure that the *Kennkarte* and the only money I have – 100 zlotys – is safe. It is hard-earned money. Night after night, I sit with Janina, unravelling a pile of old garments and, to earn a few coins, we re-use the wool and knit new clothes for the villagers.

The two of us reach the edge of the city and board a crowded tram. The bread and cheese are lost underfoot. I shiver despite the heat and my cheeks burn as I silently rehearse my story – I am a teacher from another town wanting to register. I keep repeating this until I almost believe it.

The rhythms of war – dark nights lit by flares... bombs... thundering, crashing... over and over... people running, falling, screaming... daylight... soldiers in tanks... shattered bodies, blood, broken glass, collapsed buildings...

The registration office is a surging sea of people all pressing forward to get their precious pieces of paper stamped. I am caught in the wave, fearful of losing sight of Janina, but knowing that I must appear calm. I feel the eyes of the soldiers and police boring through me.

We are shoved into a queue, unquestioning, and nudged into place with rifle barrels. There we stand, inching forward ever so slowly, staring at the feet in front of us and not daring to say a word to anyone. Those who need a toilet slip out of the queue. The rest of us are like camels.

Finally, after what seems like several long hours it is my turn. The official at the table barely looks at me as he pockets my money. He appears to study my *Kennkarte* for barely a moment, then stands and turns to walk into a back room. A scream sits in my throat, but I manage to keep quiet. My earlier bravado recedes and I become more conscious of my full bladder as panic sets in.

After what seems like forever but is probably just minutes, the official returns, pausing at the doorway to survey the scene, then in slow motion returns to his seat. He yawns widely, stretching nonchalantly and calls out for some food. Then just as slowly he shuffles his seat, straightens his uniform and pats his stripes. I am sure he knows how excruciating this is for me.

And then, without making eye contact, he stamps my *Kennkarte*. Done! So easily! I can't believe it! Now all I want is to get out, find a toilet and go home. I spot the wonderfully patient Janina.

In the street a voice calls, "Madam, wait!"

We both turn to see a short stocky Polish policeman strutting towards us. His face is a full moon with holes like a cheese – I can almost see him scratching his chicken pox. His voice grates, like a fingernail scratching sandpaper.

"So," he says, "Mohammed didn't come to the mountain, but here we are."

"What, what do you mean?"

"Why are you so pale when you see me? An old friend like me? Come on Martusia, I won't eat you."

"Ach, now I remember who you are." But I don't really like what I remember about Loshek, the sneaky son of the caretaker at my high school, especially how he would try to paw me with grubby podgy hands as I walked past, and often stood at the bottom of the stairs staring up the girls' skirts. Pfe!

"And do you also remember how you, madam, you, a junior at school, refused to dance with me at my school graduation?"

He turns to Janina, toying with his gun. "You need to go home," he hisses at her.

I slip my arm through Janina's to walk with her but he grabs my shoulder and spins me around to face him. "And where do you think you're going to, my pretty? What are you frightened of? You know, it isn't nice for someone to pretend... Actually, I don't really care if you live as a Polish peasant. That's for you to choose. But you, madam, you must go home!"

Janina is crying. "Let her come with me. Please, please, please!"

"This isn't your business!" he snarls. "You go, or I'll hand you both over..."

Passers-by stare as he forces me with Janina clinging to my arm through a dim alley into a courtyard. A caretaker approaches to check our identity, but the sight of the police uniform seems to stop him mid-sentence.

"Listen, if you won't go now, it's straight to the police station!" Loshek's voice rises and he almost spits at Janina. "Leave Martusia with me! And go!"

"Please don't cry Janina. Go home. You have a family."

I watch her leave and wonder whether this is another person I will lose forever.

As we walk, his grip is relentless.

"Don't be frightened of me. Believe it or not I've helped Jews hide. I won't do you any harm. You are blonde and blue-eyed and have always been a beautiful girl. Come on, nobody will know who you are. Are you hungry?"

"Oh yes, I'm so hungry. I left very early this morning and I was in that registration office for many hours."

"Come, we'll have something to eat. And we'll talk."

A short tram ride away we reach a large black apartment building and I stumble down the dingy staircase to a tiny apartment – a bedroom with a thin double mattress and some bedding on the floor, and a kitchen that accommodates a small table and two chairs.

"Whose place is this?" I try to sound casual.

“Oh, it’s mine. Here, sit down.” He pulls out a bottle and places two tumblers on the table.

As he slurps his vodka he makes small talk about people from his schooldays.

Then without warning he stands, pulls my scarf back and forces his fingers through my tangled curls.

“Now there’s one thing... You owe me...”

He tugs at my hair until I have to stand and look at him. Pfe, such a pig! His breath is revolting and his roaming hands are like pincers around my breasts. Why do men always want to handle my breasts? A sour taste rises from my stomach and I glance through the doorway to the bedroom at the crumpled stained bedding. A torn blouse lies discarded on the floor.

“All right.” I sound braver than I feel. “But please can I have a cup of coffee first. I’m not good like this. And, and something to eat, like you said... Maybe some bread?”

Loshek prepares coffee laced with vodka. He places it, along with a dish of dirty sugar cubes and an even dirtier spoon in front of me and he rummages in a kitchen cupboard, eventually handing me a lump of hard black bread and a small piece of even harder sausage.

I hunch over my cup, gnawing at the sausage, and in slow motion I dunk the bread into the bitter brew before sucking it.

“Where is your girlfriend?”

He looks surprised. “How do you know?”

I shrug, looking at the floor in the bedroom and we are silent for several minutes. Suddenly I hear a key scratching in the lock. A buxom young woman bounces into the apartment.

“Hello.” I try not to sound too pleased.

The woman looks at Loshek quizzically.

“Meet my friend from school. Martusia. I asked her to come in for coffee. We met in the street. We’re just finishing... I’m taking her home, then I’ll come back. Anyway, why are you home so early? How come you aren’t working? What happened?”

“I don’t have a job anymore,” the young woman says despondently. “The German officer doesn’t need me to do his washing because they are all leaving town. They say the Russians are coming."

He frowns as he digests the information and turns to me. "Come on, I'll take you home."

"You know," I say when we are in the street, "I don't have any money for the tram because Aunty was paying."

"That's all right. I'll pay. Which direction do you go?"

My stomach is churning, my head is hammering, and I don't hear much of what this awful man is saying. At the end of an unfamiliar tram line, I walk purposefully down an equally unfamiliar street, wondering what on earth to do. We turn a corner and a doctor's plaque gleams in the half-light. I want to kiss it.

"This is where I… thank you. I'm going up now… you, you can't come with me to my… Goodbye."

"Okay, I'll go, but I'll see you again soon, don't worry."

I ring the bell and rush up to an empty waiting room on the third floor. Fearfully I look out of a window and see him pacing. I have to wait.

"I have stomach pains, doctor. Please, please examine me," I say when the doctor appears. And a few minutes later, "I'm sorry. I'm so, so sorry. How can I… I have no money with me."

"That's all right," he says. "Let me have a look. Get undressed."

After a thorough examination he looks at me gravely. "You know, I can't feel anything wrong. Maybe you will need more attention, or maybe it was a passing pain, gas maybe."

Slowly I get dressed and the doctor takes my particulars. I try not to blush as I tell him a series of untruths.

'You know it is almost curfew. It isn't safe for you to go back out there. If you stay here for the night I can check if the pain has gone away in the morning. Maybe you need a little food. I will get you something."

I sense him watching me as I glance nervously out to the street. "Here, please eat something," he says gently. "If there is anything else that you need?" he offers. I murmur my gratitude for the food as I curl up on a couch at his insistence.

"Thank you so much. But I… I am so embarrassed. Please, could I borrow some money... just for the tram to get to the other side of town. I promise I will bring it as soon as I can."

"You needn't worry, whenever you can manage it," says the doctor as if he has known me for a long time and this is a normal visit.

Janina is overjoyed to see me. "How did you...? I can't believe it. I was so afraid for you."

I risk an interruption. "So Mum, is it possible the doctor was Jewish?"

"Maybe. "But you know Helen, nobody would admit such a thing at the time. Mind you, there were some Poles like Janina and Roman who were kind and helpful. But you never were knowing who was Jewish or who had a Jewish grandparent or whatever. Hitler said you needed to be Aryan for more than one generation to be 'pure'. Maybe the doctor was just a good man.

"You know, I thought I saw little nail holes by his front door, as though there had been a mezuzah on the doorpost, but maybe I was imagining it. I kept seeing mezuzah holes in so many places. It said more about who was not there anymore than who was still there."

Mum stops talking and looks up when two men in dark suits, matching pale blue shirts and fashionable ties come into the café. One waves to me, and I smile and nod in response.

"Such an elegant, good-looking man, that one who you know," Mum murmurs just loud enough for me to hear. "Why do you not invite him to come and talk to us?"

I roll my eyes, but I'm smiling. Some things never change.

"More importantly, have you finished your story?"

"Oy Helen, enough... Thinking about Poland makes me tired. You know, even after so many years, when I see an ambulance, I look for tanks. I hear loud boots and I can't help wondering if it's the SS... Ach, I'm being pathetic. Even a stupid queue... it all just comes back... And here I am in this beautiful city far, far away. But... maybe... maybe it will never go away. Now I think I need to go home, perhaps in a taxi if you are too busy to come home now."

"I need to see someone for maybe half an hour and then I can take you," I say as I blink back tears and embrace my mother.

14

ANOTHER WORLD

Melbourne 1979

"You know, Evinka, I never wanted for you to think of me as a hero. I just want for you girls to love me. As an ordinary father.

"So. Where to start ...?"

After some time at the Janowska camp we observe first one group, and then another, of maybe 150 people every three months or so, being selected carefully, then taken away, never to be seen again. At first, we wonder whether these men – the ones who seemed healthiest and with the strongest constitutions – are being taken to another camp, maybe the extermination camp, Treblinka. But that doesn't make sense. Not that anything makes sense anymore, certainly not big groups of people able to stand tall, vanishing like that.

Then one morning I find out. Roll call separates out another 150 including me, and we, the chosen, are loaded onto a truck to be driven away to a barren nondescript area outside Lvov. It is obvious that where we stand around waiting is not the real destination, unless the Germans are planning to kill us here. After waiting all day, we are returned to the camp.

By then, we are not just puzzled. We are absolutely terrified. Nobody can sleep that night and I prepare myself to die. Some of the men are so scared that they throw themselves at the electric fence rather than leave the camp. A few choose to resist the Germans, knowing it will earn them a bullet in the head. And always, the dogs are ready to pounce – and those animals have been trained to be truly vicious.

Early in the morning maybe 1,000 people, including the selected group, are shoved onto trains. Once again, the assumption is we are bound for Treblinka. *Schnell, schnell* [fast, fast], we are urged as we stumble into over-crowded carriages, a quickstep ahead of the dogs. Going to our death?

Half joking, half serious, I shake hands with my friend Kuba, an engineer whose work is always needed and is part of this group. Checking that we aren't being watched, I thrust at him my last two 20-golden dollar coins and an old watch like those used by conductors.

"I don't think I need this watch anymore. You'd better take it from me."

"Do you still think nothing can happen to you? You're still smiling."

"Smiling or not smiling, if I go, I go with a smile. If that watch stops you will know that I died."

Then strangely, each member of the selected group of 150 is called by name and ordered off the train. We are told to wait for transport and eventually we are driven away in trucks around the outskirts of the city until we reach a fenced compound with what looks like a temporary building and barracks overlooking a ravine. Nobody says a word as we wait. Wait for what? To be killed? To die falling into the ravine?

The Sonderkommando addresses us: "Fellow workers, you have been freed from all the misery that you have been through. You are going to start a new life where you will never be hungry, where you will get first class shoes, underclothes, shirts and two changes of over clothes. If you work together with me, without question, you will live forever."

The silence is accompanied by looks of disbelief. What? No gas chambers? No smoke? I wonder if they have an electric death chamber.

We continue to stand. And we wait.

Then the unbelievable happens. We are led to mounds of the cleanest clothes I have seen for a long time – shoes, boots, socks, shirts – and we are handed navy trousers, an overcoat and gloves each. When we are dressed each of us is presented with a shovel.

"You will work," we are told, "but first, eat."

I look for the usual stale bread and watery soup and can't believe what is put in front of us. It is a real meal of boiled meat, potatoes and cabbage – the same meal as the Germans are eating. It's all I can do not to gobble the food at speed. Am I hallucinating?

In the barracks there are thick sleeping bags and names of previous groups of inmates carved into the wooden floor. Someone has scratched the words *Toten Brigade* [Death Brigade] above the doorway and I wonder what that refers to. Still, to have real food, and clean clothes... that is a miracle, even if only for a short time. Eyes start to brighten.

"So Felek, if you believe in another world this is probably it," says my friend Moishe.

"If all we have is a few weeks then let's live them as best we can," I suggest. "I wonder what this is about."

We don't have long to wait. Talk in the camp from which we had been taken had been that when the German troops arrived in Lvov in 1941, they shot Jews, Ukrainians, Russians and Poles – anyone rather than be killed themselves. Gypsies and homosexuals were identified and killed too. We are told there were many bodies lying around so they were piled into pits several meters deep and covered over.

The task for us, this select group of men, is to open the pits and excavate the bodies that have been decomposing for more than two years. Valuables like gold teeth are to be extracted, and we are closely supervised to ensure that we don't take any valuables for ourselves.

For two, sometimes three days, we drag out bodies and pile the remains as high as we can. Then we follow instructions for how to add wood and petrol so nothing recognizable will remain after we set fire to the pile. When the fire dies down, we clean up what is left, the bones are crushed, and all the while we check for valuables we might have missed. Very occasionally someone might find a diamond that can be slipped into a sleeve while the nearest guard is looking the other way. Then the whole soul-destroying process begins again. There is to be no visible evidence of any wartime atrocities that occurred in Lvov.

The stench is unbearable but refusing to do the job is not an option. We are in an enclosed camp and have no idea how many sharpshooters with machine guns might be waiting outside. Sixteen people die in the first two weeks, some through illness, some taken away for the slightest infringement or hint of rebelliousness. They are shot, we learn, though surprisingly not in front of us. Two people try to run away and one of us has to hang them. That poor man will never be the same after doing such a thing; it is as if he has suffered brain damage. When the guards inform us we have to choose a *kapo*, this man volunteers to take on the unenviable task of supervising and punishing fellow prisoners on behalf of the Germans.

There are instructions that everyone must stay healthy and clean, as the Germans are afraid of disease spreading to them. Temporary showers are set up using water from the city's main water pump nearby and we use a lot of disinfectant. Clothes are taken away each day and we receive clean ones in exchange. It is so unlike the conditions we got used to in the camp. But so is the work unlike anything we could possibly have imagined.

The weeks pass and we get to know the guards, who in turn become a little less vigilant and less aggressive when they see that we work hard and don't cause trouble.

As we lie on our bunks, so overtired that we struggle to fall sleep, we talk quietly. Someone has scratched a small calendar on the wall, marking the days, and has worked out that the next night must be *Kol Nidrei*, the evening of *Yom Kippur* – a time for forgiving and asking for forgiveness. In normal times *Yom Kippur*, the Day of Atonement, is a special day of praying and fasting. Fasting? Ha! We've done plenty of that.

Moishe and I take courage in hand. In the morning, we go to the commandant and ask if we can please pray in a corner of the bunk room that night. The worst that can happen is that we won't get permission, but we don't think we would be killed for our request. Amazingly, he allows it.

Moishe, this fine educated rabbi from Vienna, who speaks beautiful Polish and flawless German, leads us in his non-Orthodox way and, remembering my yeshiva education, I am able to join him. We quietly wail the *Kol Nidrei* prayer like never before, humbling ourselves before God as we remember the prayers seeking forgiveness for our sins. We chant *Avinu Malkeinu* (our Father, our King) to give us strength and help us. But nothing is quite as painful as when we whisper *Kaddish*, the prayer for everyone we have lost. The ground is wet with our tears as we allow ourselves to remember *Kol Nidrei* of previous years.

That night my father appears in my dreams. "You will survive," he says. It is an instruction, not a prophecy. "You must do something. Remember, even if you are going to die, then die after trying, not by giving in. Never give in. You must not give in."

"What can it mean? What can we do?" I ask Moishe as we wield our shovels the next day.

"I don't know Felek, but think carefully. Maybe it is a sign, your sign for action. Maybe it is a sign for us all, for us to know that we've tried."

"But it seems futile and I want to live," I protest.

"We all die some time my friend, but maybe we should believe this is not yet our time. Because this is not really a life, which your dream is reminding us... reminding us that there can be more to life than this macabre existence in this miserable place. We need to take action."

A guard is watching us, so we continue to work in silence. I keep puzzling over why we are still here, alive after more than three months of hard work. Why haven't the Germans moved us somewhere else, or killed us and replaced us with new people, like they did before? Have they run out of able-bodied prisoners? Will I ever know?

Night-time becomes talking time, time to plan an escape, to form a group of leaders, time to work out a plan. We share information about outside contacts given to us by members of the resistance movement while we were in the bigger camp, just in case the impossible could happen. And we watch for an opportunity.

There are 59 Germans, 10 *kapos*, and a 134 prisoners. The first cold dry snow starts to fall. Standing still on two-hour watches has become an icy prospect for the guards, so they instruct two prisoners at a time to take an axe and go out into the nearby forest to cut some firewood, all the while with a machine gun trained on them. It becomes a regular routine.

Until 19 November 1943...

Two of us return to the camp with wood. The guards who have been watching from a distance light up cigarettes, losing interest once we are back inside the gate. Within a couple of minutes, we overpower the first guard. I wield the axe. I have barely a moment to look at the blood on my hands. I freeze momentarily, then grab his machine gun and swing around to kill the second guard before turning the gun onto other guards. It is the first time that I have ever held a weapon and I am unsteady for the first shot, but then adrenalin becomes my friend. This is our only chance of survival. Moishe grabs two grenades that have fallen out of the first guard's pocket and puts them to use as he rushes towards the barracks occupied by the Germans.

By this time large numbers of Germans are pouring out of the barracks shooting randomly but the prisoners are ready for them. This motley group of untrained Jews has nothing to lose and are as disciplined as any army unit. Grenades grabbed from lifeless bodies are hurled at the Germans and several die immediately. When more Germans turn to flee, we don't let them. With that first machine gun I fire blindly at soldiers who are caught unawares. Within minutes all 134 prisoners are running out of the camp – out of that stinking *Toten Brigade.* The *kapos* who have survived run in a different direction, maybe thinking they might be saved by the Germans.

It is unlikely that any of us have thought much about what will happen after we have fired those weapons. We just know we have to do it, and we know we have to run. I have no regrets.

Germans appear from everywhere. I am sure they must be pouring out of the garrison in Lvov in their thousands, accompanied by dogs. The sharpshooters who I guessed have been hiding in the forest, kill some of the escapees, including my good friend Moishe. Airplanes suddenly appear and parachutes with flares attached drop around us.

Escape seems impossible, but I run like never before, for maybe a kilometer, slipping and sliding on the frozen ground. My lungs and ears are bursting and the air bites at my throat. The typhoid fever that made me so ill a few months ago has not really left my body, and I struggle to breathe. I can hear the dogs getting closer.

When I come upon a dilapidated, snow-covered, bombed-out house I collapse just inside the doorway, unable to go any further. Beyond exhaustion and knowing that I am sick with more than fear. I sense dogs sniffing around me, but they leave me as if I am a corpse. Maybe I am really dying.

I lose track of time, of how long I have been lying here, just conscious enough to occasionally suck lumps of dirty snow. Then I hear voices speaking German which jolt me into realizing I can't stay here any longer.

That night, my skin blazing feverishly, I drag myself up and start walking, very slowly towards where I think there may be help. Somehow, I manage to walk maybe eight kilometers to a Russian church, one of the "safe" addresses where I hope I can stay. I stumble into a sheltered area in the garden, shivering and perspiring, my exposed extremities numb with cold.

A Polish gardener discovers me, and amazingly, my friend Kuba appears behind him. Miraculously he too has escaped and has come straight here. He tells me that eight days have passed since we broke out and he has no idea where anyone else is. He wonders whether we are the only survivors.

I am suffering from pneumonia and frostbite. My feet are so swollen that my boots have to be cut off and it is a miracle that I haven't lost any fingers or toes. The gardener is reluctant to let us stay for long, despite his pity, and I know that if we are caught, the Germans will show no mercy to him or us. Still, the language of diamonds – the best currency of the time – is eloquent. Despite my delirium, I remember the five gems I have kept close to my body. The gardener's attitude softens.

There is no thought of finding a doctor for me – that would be far too dangerous, but this good man does find medicine and food. He and two other Polish men build a shelter covered with a heap of coal. They make an opening for access and air and bring us food and blankets.

For five and a half months we live in the shelter with those kind Polish people keeping watch. At night when all is quiet, we climb out and walk around. I am gaining strength, but for the first time I am losing heart. There are days when I don't want to live any more. Yet that is when I hear my father's voice: "You are going to survive and you are not going to give up now."

It is easier to be more optimistic when the weather becomes warmer and we hear that the Russians have taken over Lvov. One day in May we walk out into the sunshine and leave the church, and I wonder whether I would ever be able to tell anyone what has happened.

There is a long silence.

Feliks, with the microphone still attached, struggles to leave, saying, "Let me out of here."

Someone asks, "Feliks, do you want to tell us what happened afterwards?"

"No. Thirteen of us survived..." He is breathless... sobbing as he runs out to the street...

Melbourne 2020

"Oh my God Eve! I can't believe what I've been hearing and transcribing. So much more detail than I've heard before." I look at my sister with increased admiration.

Since the premiere of Eve's film 'Man on the Bus' she has obtained a copy of the original raw video footage of Dad's studio recording now stored at the Australian Film and Sound Archive and edited for Bob Weis's documentary 'Proud to Live'.

"What an extraordinary man Dad was! It's great that you sat with him through that interview. It must have been so hard for him to talk about. No wonder he tried to run out of the interview with the microphone still attached!"

"By the way, Helen, did you know that Dad had made a statement at the German Embassy in Melbourne? Apparently, it was used at the Nuremberg Trials according to the historian Waitman Beorn."

"No, I didn't know. I'm relieved that I didn't know all this while I was growing up. It would have been such a burden. No wonder Mum and Dad fobbed off my questions and got so mad when I persisted."

"Absolutely. It drove me crazy that they wouldn't talk. I was a real pain demanding to know."

"We both were. And so unaware. They were protecting us, all the time. When I confront the facts of his survival I am amazed at what he did in self-defense. And every time I get goose bumps."

"It's a lot to digest! He was incredible, and it's such a new insight into Feliks the prisoner, the escapee ... so much more than Feliks the husband, the father, the friend, the employer ... I love him even more for his audacity and his extraordinary bravery!"

"Can you imagine how traumatized he must have been just thinking about what he had done. And after his escape, wondering whether the Germans would find him in hiding?"

'The more I think about it, the more I love him."

"Me too."

We sit quietly deep in thought. For some reason I'm thinking about Dad's funeral all those years ago. A large crowd had gathered at Temple Beth Israel. The rabbi who was a good friend of the family was away, so Eve and I chose to deliver the eulogy. For many hours well into the night we pulled Dad's story together. We hadn't known as much then as we do now, but we drew on what we remembered, writing notes, laughing, crying, splitting up the stories so we could take it in turns to speak.

I remember reading my script through tears (I think Eve was a bit more composed than me) and we alternated, talking about this man with laughing eyes and a ready smile. His *chutzpa*, his generosity, his intelligence, his business and community spirit, his courage and heroism, and above all his love for us. We lightly sketched the pre-war years and those during the war, but we drew pleasure from focusing on the new life he and Mum created in Australia – his dream come true.

When Mum died 11 years later there was no question – we would do the same for her, tears notwithstanding. Once more Temple Beth Israel filled up, the exterior facing Alma Road adorned by Mum's mural 'From Creation to Redemption'. We talked about Mum's equally extraordinary life, before, during and after the war. Beautiful, vivacious – always the life of the party – she was creative, gutsy, loving, equally intelligent and generous, a multi-linguist, vulnerable yet determined, and a wonderful mother. Despite the large number of people surrounding me at the graveside, I felt lonelier than ever as I recited Kaddish. The bond of being Mum's only possession had been severed.

15

SECRETS AND HALF TRUTHS

In 2009, when Eve and I visited Lviv (previously known as Lvov) with my partner, we found what had been the street where the Asz (Ash) family had lived. The street had been re-named, which made it hard to find, and there was no building on the site. There was little trace of the vibrant Jewish life that had once been an integral part of the city. What might we find?

Lvov 1944

When Felek emerged from hiding in May 1944, there was still the family's apartment in Ulica Sykstuska 5, although empty of his family. He reclaimed it and filled it with friends needing a place from which to start a new life. In November that year he married Martusia who, within a few weeks of the wedding, had become pregnant.

She was really unwell during her pregnancy and it was especially challenging to be sharing a room with others. In the middle of the night, she always needed to climb over four sleeping bodies to get to the tiny bathroom. If she was out and couldn't get to their apartment in time, she would race to a ground floor toilet that smelled so bad she always needed to vomit.

The apartment bathroom was filled with a pile of boxes that Felek was buying and selling, and they became another middle of the night obstacle. Of course it was Felek's fault, everyone's fault. But she knew that the inconvenience was nothing compared to what they had all been through.

One of the 13 men who had survived the escape from the Death Brigade with Felek was Mundek Gerner (Eddie in the US). He married Nina Berenstein (later Nina Zarel) and they lived in Feliks's apartment for a while before moving into a place of their own. At this time people were trying to find any relative who might have survived, however distant. Nina and Martusia discovered they had a connection – they had a common cousin Sophie, who later became a doctor and lived in the US. These were the beginnings of lifelong friendships.

When Felek decided they would move to Crakow, he went ahead of Martusia. She was left in Lvov to make her own way to Crakow once her job in a Russian supplies place came to an end.

May 1945 was the beginning of a new era of cautious optimism and hope as the war finally ended. Four months later, Martusia and Felek's baby Helena was born. Felek's business activities were a mystery to his wife. There was a moment when Martusia was in hospital and Helena was born and he came rushing into the ward clutching a case full of money and responded to questions about it with his usual shrug and, "Don't worry darling." He obviously didn't want to involve her.

Meanwhile Mundek and Nina had left Lvov and were also living in Crakow. They were exceptional friends. When Felek's fortunes fluctuated, he needed to borrow money to buy a pram for his baby. Mundek, who had been able to save a little money from his wages, generously emptied out his bank account and bought the pram. After all they had been through together, he felt this beautiful baby was a shared gift of hope for a better future.

Another escapee, Kuba and his wife Guta, lived and worked with Felek for some time. Eight months after Helena was born, they had a son, Anatol. When Guta struggled to feed her baby Martusia became Anatol's wet nurse and fed both babies.

This was another of Mum's stories that she loved to share, along with how she bathed me in a bidet. Imagine my amazement in 2020 when Anatol, living in Canada, contacted Eve and me, the connection being made through seeing Eve's documentary "Man on the Bus." It provided an opportunity to connect us, his family story with ours, and we remain "bosom buddies."

Crakow 1946

Felek came rushing up the stairs and flung open the door.

"Oh, good that you are here Tusia. We have to leave quickly. I was stopped in the street today and warned that I must enlist in the army in one week's time. It's good they didn't take me straight away." He breathed heavily.

"You know, I have no *koyekhh* to fight. Or to live with abusive behavior against Jews in the army. And you can imagine the primitive conditions. Enough already!"

"For goodness' sake, Felek. Going with a baby?"

"We must, *kochanie,* my darling, and the others will come too.

"Some of these men, they saved my life in the camp, they looked after me when I had typhoid fever. Can you imagine I survived such an illness when everyone else either died from it, or was shot because they had caught it! I'm alive only because of them. I told you how when we escaped from the Nazi guards, I caught pneumonia, and it was Kuba who suddenly appeared and arranged for blankets and some food after I hadn't eaten for so many days and could hardly move. Can you imagine what a risk everyone took. We have to look after each other. There is no question."

Two days after Felek was warned about army service, Martusia returned from her usual walk in the park with Helena in the pram, to find the boxes in the bathroom had gone. Felek was there, flushed with excitement. "We can go," he announced, "I sold all the boxes and look what I bought instead."

She stared in disbelief at the exquisite sparkling booty. "I don't ... don't understand. What have you done?"

"I met a Pole who needed boxes. He had no idea what these were worth, so I bargained with him. He got his boxes and now we have international currency. We can go anywhere with these."

She was panic-stricken. "You're crazy. Where will we go? How can we cross the border without proper papers?" She fired questions like bullets and Felek looked a little shame-faced.

"I have papers. Look!"

"Felush, for goodness' sake, how could you? You have made me older and not even the right birthday!"

"I had to make myself older – to say I was born in 1903 not 1911 so I wouldn't be eligible for the army or they would stop me at the border. So I thought it better to make you older too," he explained with a wry smile. "I'm sorry, but you know how it's not easy to get these papers."

Had he forgotten her details and needed to write something quickly? It was odd, she thought, he was right with her birth year. But not the month. The papers she had been using during the latter part of the war had made her younger than she really was. Now he was making her almost her proper age. How stupid of him! Still, what was the truth, and who would know, or care? There was no one left who might remember.

"There is one more thing before we can leave. We need to hide these treasures so the border guards won't find them or they are sure to confiscate them. Have you any idea how?"

She thought for a few moments, then held out her hand, smiling conspiratorially at their baby daughter. She knew exactly where to put the diamonds.

The following morning, while sitting in the park, she was thinking about the wonderful hats her Mama made before the war. She pulled out some wool and a crochet hook, and at great speed, she made a beautiful lacy bonnet adorned with a row of flowers. Her baby would be more precious than ever.

Later when Felek asked, "What did you do?" she shook her head and put a finger to her lips. "Shush, if you don't know, you can't say the wrong thing. This is my secret."

There was little to pack and they made their way to the station with their friends without delay. As the train approached the border

Felek presented their papers. He had confidently handed over his last zlotys to pay for the tickets. Now he had just a few koruna, the Czechoslovakian currency he had managed to buy. Martusia didn't ask how.

There were surprisingly few questions from the border guards, one of whom was especially charmed by Helena. He plucked her from her mother's arms and encouraged her to play with the buttons on his uniform. As Helena's bonnet started to slip Martusia watched in alarm. Without thinking, she flashed a flirtatious smile and retrieved her child, while clutching the bonnet firmly. At which point Helena started to wail loudly.

"My darling precious Heleninka, you must learn not to play with strange men," she crooned as she cradled her baby's head.

When they were safely in Prague, Felek found a room on the second floor of a building near the center of the city and their companions moved into another. The building was full of Jews leaving Poland.

Helena cried a lot, and Martusia guessed that her milk no longer satisfied her baby. Luck had been on her side until now, and she was grateful that she had had little trouble feeding both her baby and Guta's. But now she wondered what she could find to give Helena. She boiled some wilted spinach leaves, thickened the spinach water with flour and fed her the glue-like mixture. The next day she grated a carrot and squeezed out the juice as best she could, realizing that she could thicken this too. Helena ate greedily.

When the time came for Felek to sell a diamond, Martusia carefully unpicked the center of one of the flowers in the bonnet.

"Oy, how wonderful you are Tushinka! I am so lucky to be married to such a clever woman!"

Prague was a haven and they stayed for several weeks, enjoying the beauty of the city which, like Crakow, had escaped the bombing. The diamond had turned out to be worth enough for Felek to feel generous. For the first time since before the war they could spend a little money on more than just essentials. Martusia set her heart on some beautiful cake forks and pleaded with him to let her buy them. All he could think of was having them confiscated at the border, but she was adamant that the treasures would be out of sight.

"Please Tusia, they will check the pram."

"I know. Leave it to me."

Sure enough, at the Czech border, the border guard asked if they had anything to declare. "Nothing, kind sir," she assured him, flaunting her linguistic flair and her most alluring smile. After a thorough check of their possessions, including the pram, they were waved on to continue the long journey.

It wasn't until they were alone in their room in Paris that she unbuttoned her coat and from inside her bra she extracted 12 sharp little cake forks and a pair of serving utensils. Felek burst into a fit of uncontrollable laughter, declaring nothing had been so funny for so many years.

"How smart can you be with hiding paper money?" he asked the next day. "I now have big paper francs and it isn't safe to carry so much money. Some of it belongs to the others as well."

"Give me the money and I will find somewhere." He knew not to ask anything more.

Every day Martusia would bounce the pram down four flights of stairs, then go for a walk through the beautiful cobbled streets and into the park. Back at the apartment she would hoist the heavy pram back up the stairs.

The concierge took pity on her. "Madame, I can find a place downstairs where you can leave the pram and give you a cot for your little Helena."

"Thank you so much Madame," she replied in near fluent French, "but my baby will only sleep in the pram and would wake everyone in the building if we put her in a different bed."

"As you wish, Madame, but while you are in the park I will put a cot in your room for her, just in case."

And check all my possessions, no doubt, thought Martusia, relieved that she had found a safe place for the money. She dragged the pram upstairs yet again and checked the tubular handle for the tenth time that day. She was happy to put up with the inconvenience of the stairs while they lived in Paris, which turned out to be for two months.

Melbourne 1994

My latest trip to Melbourne coincides with Mum's scheduled medical appointment. Eve and I are terribly worried about Mum's persistent coughing fits every day. This has gone on for years and seems to be getting worse. Our fear is that she could choke to death while having one of her prolonged coughing fits.

We ask the doctor for options, none of which sound encouraging.

"What would you do if it was your mother?" Eve asks.

"Definitely a tracheotomy," he replies.

Later Eve and I take it in turns to explain to our reluctant mother how much better she will feel after the operation, and how her quality of life will improve.

"You know, Helen, I was right," Mum says hoarsely after the operation. She needs to put a finger over a newly installed tube to produce a sound, which is taking some getting used to.

"The Germans and the Russians, and the Ukrainians – they were all terrible, but they didn't kill me like this tube will. This is definitely the worst thing," she says coughing.

In her own bed in her apartment, she lies back against her pillows, exhausted from this new and different cough. She claims she doesn't know which she hates more – the endless coughing of the past years or struggling to breathe with an irritating tube in her neck. It's hard to believe someone who was so creative and energetic, so full of life, is the same person. It breaks my heart to hear her say, "Oy darling, I am perpetually tired, and suffering so much."

I watch her as she plays with her lovingly prepared dinner. She is in no hurry – it's too painful to eat. And it hurts me to watch her. I can hear her admonitions as I was growing up: "Eating up, finishing everything. When you are living through a war you are not knowing when you will be getting food again, so you always eat everything."

"Fast," I would add, laughing, watching Dad at mealtimes. He never learned to eat slowly, except when he was in hospital, dying. Even then he gulped the chicken soup I would bring him.

I remove Mum's barely eaten food she usually enjoys.

There's little relief for Mum from the congestion that is causing her so much discomfort. The surgeon thinks that it's aggravated by the scar tissue that has built up in her trachea. All I can see is that the tracheotomy appears to make little difference. This isn't the quality-of-life she was promised.

'Let's watch a video, Mum. You've got a few here."

"That is a good idea. You know Helen, there is a video of me being interviewed. I have never shown it to you because you are never here for long en..." she rasps, before being consumed by a coughing fit.

After her evening cocktail of pills, we settle down to watch. She soon begins to snore lightly so, careful not to wake her, I gently prise the remote control from her clenched fist, turn off the light and continue to watch.

Startled by what I'm hearing, I stop the video and replay a segment. I'm mystified by what Mum is saying. Who is this interviewer? It's extraordinary how much she tells her, a stranger, and in so much more detail than she has ever been prepared to tell me, and probably Eve. This is a chapter of her life that's new to me.

What's all this stuff about the pre-war years? Working in another town for a lawyer? Debt-collecting? And what labor camp? Is this all true? Did she tell us a whole lot of compressed stories about her life so we'd never know her age? I do some hasty arithmetic and realize that maybe we should have celebrated, or at least recognized, her 79th birthday earlier in the year, not her 75th.

I tiptoe to another room and ring my sister.

"Hi Eve, got a few minutes?"

As always Eve is working into the night, but she's happy to stop and talk.

"There's something odd. I've been watching a video where Mum talked to an interviewer. Has she ever shown it to you?"

"Actually, no. As far as I can remember, I think I knew about it but

I assumed that we'd been told whatever she might tell anyone else. From the tone of your voice, I was wrong. Sounds like it could be different from all those research tapes Jenny Pausacker recorded back in the '80s."

"Well, I'm absolutely sure that Mum has never told me about going off to work in another town before the war. I had no idea. She just blurred that time in her life. Did she ever tell you anything?"

"Nope. But it does go to show how often she's been only half honest with us. And all those years when we were kids, she insisted we always tell the truth. Ha! So tell me more about the video that I haven't seen."

I faithfully recount what I've learned about working for a lawyer, doing menial office work, debt-collecting on his behalf.

"You're kidding! So why keep that a secret?"

"Well, we might have to settle for the cute stories we know, like when I was a baby and she hid diamonds in my bonnet. I wonder how many secrets and half-truths Mum has been clinging to."

The next day I offer to help Mum with her complicated morning routine until the caregiver arrives. She's determined to manage the lengthy process alone and it's exhausting her. I help her clear the thick, dull green sputum from the tube in her throat, then watch her undress and shower, ever so slowly. When the time comes to change the colostomy bag (which she has had for so many years since she was diagnosed with ulcerative colitis – the operation wasn't reversible back then), she shoos me out of the bathroom and proceeds to dress and perfume herself. After nearly half an hour she returns to the bedroom and slides gratefully into her bed before swallowing another round of pills. She has slept fitfully during the night and I can see that she is tired and in pain. Even eating a soft-boiled egg is a struggle.

'This bloody tube is driving me crazy! I am hating it!" Mum says, pushing the breakfast tray away.

I fight back tears as I watch her tie a brightly colored scarf around her neck before casually applying her usual asymmetric smudges of eye shadow and a bright red approximation of her lips. Applying makeup has always been a casual process, but she is unsurpassed at making a good impression, especially for a professional man.

The doctor arrives. “How are you today, Martha?” he asks.

“How I am? I am fine,” she says as clearly as possible after slipping her finger under the scarf. And she flashes her beautiful smile.

16

VIOLETS AND LILY OF THE VALLEY

Auckland 2009

Eve is visiting on one of her trips between Melbourne and her work in LA.

"You know, I've been thinking how I wish we could fill in more of the missing pieces of Mum and Dad's wartime stories," I start.

"Yeah, me too."

"What do you think about going to Poland? To Warsaw, Lvov – or Lviv as it is now... Zloczow, Crakow... see what's left of the camp at Janowska... the key places we know about."

"Well Mum and Dad never wanted to go back and they've been dead all these years. I'm wondering how come you're suddenly telling me you want to go to Zloczow and Lviv which are in bloody Ukraine now."

The idea hasn't come completely out of the blue. One of Mum's school friends, Gina Neustein, had migrated from Zloczow to Sydney and kept in touch when I was growing up. Recently her son, Michael has come to Auckland with his New Zealand wife and we meet when I am (unusually) attending the Orthodox synagogue. Michael and Janet are here to commemorate her father's *yahrtzeit*.

My arts practice has extended to designing *Judaica* – ritual objects for synagogues, and I had been commissioned to produce a Torah curtain which is being revealed to the community. I am here with my colleague Freda Brierley who has worked on the curtain with me. Over sweet wine and *challah* after the service Michael and I catch up animatedly.

"We're going to Zloczow. You should come too," he announces. "A memorial for the Jews who were killed in the 1941 pogrom is being unveiled in the forest on the edge of Zloczow." My eyes widen. Commemorating my grandmother? Mum's first husband?

He promises to email me details of the group going – from Israel, US, Canada, France, Australia – all descended from Jews who lived in Mum's small town. There would be a bus, and my partner and I could be part of a group booking. And, of course, Eve should come too.

For a moment I am silenced. This isn't what I had expected but somehow it fits with what I had been vaguely thinking.

Eve isn't sure whether she will join us since she has another trip planned. Maybe she can fit it in. I am definite that I want to go. Eve is making a film, a personal documentary that is well under way and she has already cut a trailer for it. She always carries a movie camera to record anything that might be relevant and I suggest that Poland and Ukraine would be useful. "I'm wondering if we might learn more, get a sense of the place, maybe have a better understanding of our background. It feels like we've got some really interesting pieces of information. And if we knew more, it might help our kids understand us better as well. I'm sure we've all been affected by the stuff Mum and Dad wouldn't tell us.

"And… I'm really not sure, except there's a nagging thought that if we don't go now, we might never go. When I think about it, it's crazy I've never been back to my birth place. Ukraine is hardly my first choice for an overseas trip, but it feels important. Besides it's a good opportunity with all these other people going. Who would have thought there would be enough of us with Zloczow heritage to fill a bus. I have a feeling that I need to go. It's such unfinished business. Please come with me."

"I didn't realize you so desperately wanted to do this. Yes, I'll come. Send me the itinerary and I'll try to join you somewhere. I'll talk to you from LA. Just give me enough time to organize things. Love you lots."

"Love you too."

My mind turns to things like how we will manage the languages. Our Polish is pretty ropey, Ukrainian non-existent, although Eve did learn Russian at school. So she might be able to read some street signs in Ukraine. I guess we'll have to use interpreters.

Flying into Kyiv (which we knew as Kiev) feels strange and I'm glad the arrangement is to meet the other people on the tour at the hotel. They turn out to be a really interesting group, speaking English with a variety of accents and luckily some able to speak Polish. Charming Nobel Laureate Roald Hoffman is one of the group and I can't help thinking there must have been so many amazing people just from Zloczow who were lost during the war.

Michael and Janet Neustein's son, an architect like his father, has found the Pinchuk Art Centre in Kyiv where we have time to visit 'Requiem', an impressive major retrospective of Damien Hirst's artworks. It is a strange prelude to all that awaits us.

Fortunately during the bus trip there are some hilarious moments that balance out the tragedies that unfold. Like the day the New Yorkers and Israelis have an intense voluble serious argument about when to have lunch. We enjoy the entertainment.

On the first morning we set out on the first leg of the 550 kilometers to Lviv. Our initial stop at Babi Yar – that infamous ravine where more than 30,000 Jews were massacred in two days – provokes the first of many tears that recur whenever we recite Kaddish. And each time we pause at yet another memorial, we repeat Kaddish.

There are few Jews in the villages we pass through. Breakfast in an orphanage in Zhitomir, and visiting synagogues in places like Berdicze, Merjibusz and Midzibasz, remind us of the Jewish life that once existed and has all but disappeared. But not quite. One of the Israelis asks of a religious Jew we meet: "Why do you stay here? How can there be a Jewish life? Why don't you come to Israel?" The sobering answer is: "Because if we leave, they will have won."

Eve joins us in Lviv. She has booked into The Grand Hotel. It's really old and we talked about how it would have been there when our parents were living there. I remember Dad telling me that the Germans used to call the city Lemberg. It's tragic how many wars there have been, fighting over the territory. As part of winning and showing who is in charge, the winners re-name streets, towns and cities. And all the time it's the people who suffer.

Lvov – where after leaving Warsaw, Dad's family lived at *Ulica Syktuska 5* and built up a business manufacturing and selling shoes. We locate the now empty site – the apartment building had still been there when Dad emerged from hiding after his daring escape from the *Toten Brigade*.

Lvov – where most of the whole family, more than 100 members of the Asz family, lost their lives... except Dad...

Lvov – Janowska, on the outskirts of this city, is located by Kleparov station, and is the concentration camp from which Dad escaped...

Lvov – where Felek/Feliks met Martusia/Martha, and convinced her to marry him...

Janowska – a sad neglected overgrown place, now housing a prison, with an apology for a memorial at its entrance. Outside the gate, with my sister at my side, tears flow as we recite Kaddish in memory of the grandparents, aunts, uncles and a baby cousin we have never known.

Zloczow is about 70 kilometers from Lvov. We receive an unexpected invitation to share a 10 a.m. toast with the mayor to celebrate the town's anniversary. He seems surprised and pleased to see us as no one else has turned up, and he has obviously not waited before having his first drink.

Later we pace slowly along the tree-lined main street and I am lost in thought. Mum once described its beauty, comparing it to Collins Street in Melbourne, although I'm not so sure. But then, my memory has been known to fool me – maybe it's a trait I inherited from her.

Which was the balcony that the young Martusia would lean over to talk to a good-looking engineer, the man she truly loved and married all those years ago? We can't work out which is her mother's apartment, but we do find Mum's nondescript old school with its tiny windows, and the gloomy looking police station which now serves as a council office. And we recall Mum's story about her best friend who handed Jews over to the Nazis, and others with whom she was neither particularly close, nor had any expectations – they were hiding Jews, caring for them.

In a wooded area on the edge of the town stands a new memorial in memory of the Jews killed during the fateful pogrom of 1941. Because I hadn't known about the making of the memorial soon enough, our grandmother's name is missing, as are many others. But in my heart Zanetta Wagner's name is there. As is Leon Siegel's, Mum's first husband. At the somber morning event to unveil the memorial, we stand among the trees with a small number of Zloczow residents and local dignitaries. Our busload recites Kaddish once more and we sing the Jewish partisan song. As always, Eve is filming.

We are taken to Sobiewski Castle, a popular location for wedding photos and happy events. There is a presentation by a historian that disturbs Eve and me. The information he relays is that only men were killed in the pogrom that ended in the Sobiewski grounds – a very different story from the one Mum had told an interviewer about her mother's fate. Eve finds another onsite historian who tells us we are wrong. No Jews were killed in the castle grounds – but maybe outside the walls.

We are confused and upset. We have so many questions that we decide to take another day trip to Janowska and to Zloczow.

Eve hires a car with an interpreter, Igor, as well as a driver. Arriving near Janowska, we approach the camp, not from the gate where we had stopped at the memorial the previous day, but down a fairly steep back road. Slowly we drive past what looks like a graveyard of rusting machinery and vehicle parts, and the end of an old railway track. We are surprised to see a caretaker appear from a dilapidated shed – an old man with a goitre on his neck, accompanied by a pair of scrawny dogs. He steps out quickly and waves us down. Igor explains why we are here and the driver is instructed to take the car partway up the road bordered by barbed wire.

Meanwhile the caretaker has decided we are harmless, and is pleased to talk to us as he leads us through long grass and weeds until we overlook a forested area and a ravine. How many bodies were thrown down there? Is this where so many ran when they broke out of the camp? Is this where the German sharpshooters were waiting on the day of the breakout? And which was Dad's escape route? That prison in the distance – is that where the barracks were? And most troublesome of all, where were the bodies dug up, and then burned by Dad and the rest of the *Toten Brigade* in order to cover up Nazi crimes?

There are probably human bones under our feet we are told. I look down, shivering despite the heat. My bare legs start to itch and a rash develops. That evening Eve tells me her legs are itching too.

We return to the Sobiewcki Castle and walk around the grounds.

"It feels strange being here, Helen. We know that this castle museum was a prison and was where one of Mum's uncles worked. It's where Mum as a child played in the garden with some of the women inmates. The guidebook says there were mass executions here in 1941. So this must be where our grandmother died and likely where Mum's first husband was buried along with all those other innocent people. I feel sick thinking about it."

"It's where they were brutally murdered. By the Germans and their collaborators, who, from what I can understand, were Ukrainians."

"Yeah. And all for no reason, other than being Jewish. Jews had lived here for centuries. And in such a short time... so many dead... of unnatural causes. I want to scream it out so everyone can hear."

"This elegant green expanse of lawn with charming flower beds around the edges, it's built over human remains, again – the bones of thousands of people. It looks so benign, so attractive... and it's really weird... I bet the Ukrainians aren't too keen to share the full story of this tourist attraction. If they even know."

"Remember Mum's tape you transcribed – she described that pogrom. I've got it on my laptop and checked it again last night. I couldn't understand what that historian Marco was talking about when he said that the women and children were made to watch and then were sent home."

"I wonder if he was referring to the shooting of the Ukrainians by the Soviets days before the Germans arrived."

"Mmh. From what I understood, and I could be wrong, there were two killings – the second one was the slaughter of Jews. Likely by Ukrainians. And maybe Germans."

"You could be right, if we believe Mum's version. That historian based his theory on the testimonials of one or two people who likely escaped from the first shooting. But we've got another testimonial, if you could call Mum's tapes that... Oh damn him for creating this confusion for our whole group of second generation survivors. How will we ever really know the truth! And you know, despite Mum's fictions and fabrications over the years – and there were a few of those – I really think this part of her story rings true... I believe this is where probably Leon, and definitely our grandmother, are buried."

"You know, Helen, I think we need to really listen to Mum's and Dad's tapes again. It's as though we block out details and the pain of it all every time we listen to them, so we never really hear the complete stories.

"I'm sure Mum's mother's stories are embedded in those tapes. I need to revisit them."

Zloczow 1916

It is exceptionally cold – outside it is several degrees below zero when I slip Tusia into a warm bath. Each splash of water quickly becomes icy cold. I wrap my uncomplaining baby in a towel that has been heated in front of the fire and then embrace my gorgeous daughter inside my coat.

Marek comes to kiss us. "Goodbye my darling Zanetta and my beautiful little Martusia. I will miss you."

The Polish army is at war and his company is leaving again. As always, I wish he wouldn't go but I know he must, so I keep my thoughts to myself, not wanting to burden him. It's something Papa has impressed on me: "Zanetta, *moja kochana*, listen to me my darling, the last words before your husband goes away with the army, or anywhere, should always be good words. Just in case..."

Mother and Father are full of such admonitions – in case – and I listen, but often with a sigh once they are out of earshot. They are so old fashioned.

When I fall in love with Marek, he, bare-headed and lightly dressed on a summery Saturday morning, cycles towards our house and as always slows down to talk to me. I know that Papa is about to leave for synagogue and I nervously urge Marek to move on quickly. Too late.

Papa steps out of the house wearing his permanent frown under the wide black fur-trimmed hat he always wears, even in summer, and the lines on his brow tighten even further when he sees who I am talking to. He mutters '*gut shabbos*', his long side curls catching in the breeze as he strides out briskly. The flaps on his black coat bounce with every step, making me think of my father as an eagle. Or a bat. And I know it is pointless to argue with an eagle. Or a bat.

How unfair that my parents disapprove of Marek and his assimilated ways when I love him so much! His small dog follows him everywhere and at the sound of the dog's bell, I find a million excuses to go outside to catch a glimpse of him, to wave to him if he can't stop.

When he goes to Czechoslovakia on holiday with his family, he sends me romantic postcards, beautiful views he has painted using watercolors. Each card depicts two people walking together. In love. Like I am with him. I cherish the times we spend together, always with a chaperone. For three years I beg and plead, and wait for my parents to relent and give their permission for us to get married.

"Be careful, Zanetta," my father admonishes. "I hope you won't be punished for such stubbornness. This is not what God wants for you, nor what we want for you either, but I can see that you won't give in."

"But do I have your blessing, Papa?"

"Only because I love you and you should get married. Soon. Marek is not a bad man and I can see that he loves you. It's a pity he doesn't love God a bit more."

We have a traditional wedding under a *chuppah* - a beautiful white linen canopy that Papa has organized, me in an exquisite white dress and veil that Mama has made. The wedding is full of joy.

After five months I become pregnant. We are so happy when our daughter is born. It is such a wonderful time for the whole family. Then one day, I am walking down a staircase in my parents' home, carrying my lively six-months-old Lilka who playfully grabs my hair; I become distracted and lose my balance...

How could I fall like that? And how could I not protect my darling baby, to stop her from bumping her head so hard? My injuries are nothing when I realize that our gorgeous, gorgeous Lilka who has brought so much joy to us is no longer with us.

Marek and I are bereft and I weep every day for more than a year, until I feel movement once more, with the promise of another baby. Martusia makes us smile again. She is the center of our lives and I want nothing more than to be with her and Marek, and to surround this baby with love and blessings.

One day, after Marek has been away for two lonely months, months when I have missed him so much and prayed for his safe return, an army messenger arrives. He hands me a piece of paper. My hands shake as I read the first words over and over, and I wail in agony as the message sinks in: 'We regret to inform you... suffered from dysentery... died..."

A black veil covers my life. The dull ache of loss only lifts when I am with Tusia, when I dress her and sing her to sleep. Only my little daughter saves me from giving up. At night I lie awake, re-living every precious moment of my life with the man I adored. Had we deserved the small pieces of love we shared? Was I being punished for marrying him?

Family members help at first but they have no words that can console me. The rabbi visits, as does his wife, and as is Jewish custom, she tries to encourage me to marry again. Soon. But all I want to do is to sit at the window, Tusia in my arms, as if waiting for Marek to come home. But I know I can't keep sitting and dreaming, and it doesn't take long before I realize that with no pension from the army, I need to earn money to support us. The trouble is I'm not sure where to start.

One day, as I stare down at a passing parade in the street, the view below gives me an idea. I go to a wooden chest where I keep small pieces of fabric and start to arrange some felt in different combinations. I give some to Tusia to play with and while my daughter tries to chew the fabric I start to cut, pin and stitch.

The first cloche hat I make is a clumsy attempt. It has a strange bump at the top and doesn't fit well on my head. Late in the evening, while Tusia is asleep, I pull the hat apart and make it twice more until it hugs my head the way it should. When I finally get the shape right, I embroider flowers around the edge, mainly to cover my mistakes.

The next day, when my sister-in-law visits me, I show her the hat. She likes it so much that she insists on buying it immediately. Later that day, when she goes out for her usual walk and cup of tea with friends, she shows off her new acquisition.

With the money I earn from that unexpected first sale, I buy some fabric, and so the business begins. Zloczow women – their vanity and competitiveness – are my godsend. After a few months, some of the wealthiest and most elegant women in town beat a trail to my home to order hats. Sometimes they bring fabric to match an outfit and give me instructions that their hat must be more beautiful and exotic than anyone else's.

I'm surprised how much I enjoy making these hats. It has never occurred to me I could be a milliner. My favorite task is the embellishment – the embroidery, feathers, delicate lace and sparkling beads that have to be lavish and glamorous enough to satisfy the fussiest of women. Day and night I stitch and re-stitch.

After a year, so many people have been coming to the apartment that I decide to rent a small shop nearby. The shop becomes a success and not long after I expand the business into a second shop next door. From there I sell exclusive imported cosmetics and glamorous haberdashery, employing two young women to help me.

I also employ a nursemaid to look after Tusia while I work. My little darling, with her mop of blond curls and mischievous blue eyes, becomes quite a talker and very adventurous. She is so delightful when for my birthday she comes running to me, clutching a tiny bouquet of violets and lily of the valley and thrusts them at me. I have so much love for her.

One day, the nursemaid comes into the shop to speak to me and Tusia runs out to play on the footpath. After a few minutes I step out to check on my three-year-old, to give her a quick hug. But there's no sign of her.

Such panic! Everyone in the street starts looking for her and I run to the police station for help. Nobody knows where she is. After what seems like a very long time, a carriage pulls up outside the shop and three Polish officers step out. One lifts my child out. I grab her, but she seems unperturbed.

"What happened?" I ask through tears of relief.

Somewhat shamefaced the officers admit to chatting to Tusia when they saw her playing and she had followed them to their station. They offered her something to eat, which, they tell me, she has eaten with exceptional manners, and she seemed very content. But they realized someone would be missing the child so they brought her back.

"How could you be so thoughtless? She is all I have!" My relief turns to anger, prompting my daughter to dissolve into tears. The men murmur their apologies and leave. How could they know just how precious she is to me?

Rosh Hashanah, Yom Kippur, Succos, Simchas Torah, Chanukah... Purim, Pesach... the holidays roll around, often celebrated at my brother's home or with Marek's brothers. They rarely want to come to me for these meals, so sometimes I prepare dinner for the second night of some of the festivals and invite people who have nowhere to go. We always have a crowded table and at an early age Tusia learns how to cook and be a hostess.

One brother-in-law is the head gardener at the Sobiewski Castle, named after the Polish king who won the war with the Tartars in Vienna. The castle has been transformed into a jail and sometimes

Tusia is taken by this kind relative to play in its garden. One day when she comes home, she tells me how she likes helping some of the women inmates who are allowed to work in the garden. I feel a momentary sense of panic and want to forbid it, but decide not to say anything as I am, in fact, proud of my daughter's helpfulness.

Another of my brothers-in-law has no children and treats Tusia as though she is his adopted daughter. He is very generous which makes it hard to understand why she doesn't like visiting him. He pays for her piano lessons and asks nothing of me in return, so I'm really grateful. When she goes to his home during holidays, she comes home wearing very adult clothes for a ten-year-old. He obviously has no idea what is suitable for a young girl. I don't mind the ski equipment, but dresses with deep necklines! What does he think he's doing? Most surprisingly, Tusia invariably arrives home in a bad mood, despite being so spoilt. It doesn't make sense to me, but she never gives me an explanation.

My parents have lived on a small farm on the outskirts of Zloczow for a number of years. Tusia loves to visit as she has always adored her grandparents and has felt so free there. The love has been mutual and my father has learned to smile at last. It's such a pity that he died of a heart attack when his granddaughter was only seven years old. Meanwhile the old tensions between Mamushka and me have faded, and she comes to live with us, until pneumonia takes her life four years later.

My mother's death brings back the sadness of earlier losses. Once again, I am dependent on Tusia, but my daughter is reaching an age when she wants to push me away, as I did with my mother.

As a 12-year-old my daughter is developing into a beautiful young woman when I meet Kobe. He isn't the first man to be sent by the matchmakers, but he is the most appealing man to have courted me since Marek died. Kobe is a professor and teaches in the high school – a charming generous man, a bit younger than me, and he is exceptionally fond of Tusia.

"Why won't you marry him?" she asks when I send him away.

"You need to understand men," I try to explain to her. "He would marry me but it would be you that he will look at and want. Imagine if he is your stepfather, living under the same roof as you. Imagine if… darling, I could never forgive myself if anything happened. You matter more than anything." Tusia nods, and although she looks slightly uncomfortable, she seems to understand, showing wisdom beyond her years.

One wintry night a neighbor bangs on my door shouting, "Fire is sweeping through both shops!" When the fire brigade eventually arrives, the firemen pull down steel doors to gain access. But the water pipes outside the building are frozen so they can't hose the flames. All anyone can do is to stare helplessly. Nothing can be saved. The next day the nightmare becomes total despair when I realize that my insurance had ran out before the fire.

I am sick with worry, debilitated from vomiting and suffering terrible headaches. The doctor says it could be a result of the smoke, and he prescribes bed rest for several weeks. Once again, I agonize about how I will care for my daughter and myself. The only good thing is that Tusia takes charge of running the household, which is quite a responsibility for someone so young. Only the fact that she does it so well makes me less anxious.

Eventually I start working again, and this time I make wedding dresses and evening gowns with unique headgear to match. But I don't get the same enjoyment from my work as I used to.

In the meantime, my daughter becomes more interested in helping me and going out with friends than doing her schoolwork. I despair, not knowing what to do when she shows such defiance. All the same, I love it when she makes organza flowers to match my clients' garments. She is so inventive, using gelatine to stiffen delicate fabric which she wraps around a knitting needle to make petals.

My biggest worry is that she is becoming a beautiful spirited young woman, and at the same time she is becoming such a flirt. I am petrified that it could end badly, and before long I have reason to worry.

When Tusia is 14 years old, she earns some money by playing the piano as an accompanist to violin students from a music school. One day, the mother of one of these students comes to tell me that her son wants to get engaged to her. Engaged! At 14! What can the woman be thinking? Has Tusia encouraged him? Are boyfriends just sport for her?

The boy, a 19-year-old who has been serving in the army, is going overseas to study and he wants to get engaged before he goes. His mother likes the idea and has agreed with him that Martusia is the girl for him. My eyes are as if on stalks as I repeat, over and over, that I will not allow it.

After a year or so, the young man abandons his studies, rises to officer status in the army and asks to be transferred back to Zloczow. While Tusia is at school, he comes to see me to tell me that if she won't marry him, he will kill her and then himself. This madness makes me frantic with worry. In desperation I rush to my friend, who has become the chief of police, to ask if he has any influence to get him transferred immediately as my daughter is at risk. Luckily, he is willing to help me, or I wouldn't know what to do. It is such a relief when he agrees and the young man leaves Zloczow.

One day, a poor neighbor comes to the door. Her little boy is in bed, too cold to go to school and she is desperate. I don't have any money to give her but feel so sorry for them. Compared to her we have such riches. The only thing I can think of are Tusia's ski boots, the ones her uncle bought for her.

After school, when she comes home to get her boots to go cross-country skiing with her friends, I suggest with some difficulty, that we give the boots to the neighbor. "Listen darling, maybe you can borrow some boots from a friend or you won't go skiing for a while, but this little boy has nothing to wear. Don't you feel sorry for him like I do? Maybe you can imagine that you are sick – then you wouldn't go skiing. I'm so sorry, but I really think we should help them. He will be able to stuff the boots with paper and later grow into them. Darling, I know the boots were a gift from your uncle."

I watch her face cloud over as she silently walks away and I pray that my daughter learns to be generous, to be a willing giver. It reminds me of her struggle the first time when, after cooking a lot of food with me, we took most of it to the orphanage. I see her wrestling with herself when it comes time to hand over something special.

I worry about her a lot. Like when she goes to the children's court that manages some funds left to her for her education, money I am not allowed to touch. The money is from her father's brothers who inherited properties from their parents and decided to give some to Tusia. I don't trust the youthful good-looking man in charge at the court. Maybe it's the way he looks at her. He often asks her, a high school student, to come and see him by herself. It really doesn't feel right, but we need the money.

Tusia matriculates at the *gymnasium*, the academic high school, and sets her heart on studying fine art, but the education fund has run out. I have nothing for a dowry, so my family begin to put pressure on me for her to get married to someone who won't expect anything. But my willful daughter chooses instead to get a job with a lawyer in a nearby small town where she works in the office and as a debt collector, and stays there until her employer is called up to serve in the army.

I am so pleased when she returns. For the first time in my life, I have been living completely alone, with just my small dog for company. But Tusia is no longer the girl who went away, and I look at this poised young woman with pride and fear. She finds work helping in a shop and before long she falls in love with a lovely man, an engineer. I pray that Leon loves her too, and that she doesn't end up discarding him like a pair of old gloves as she has done with so many boyfriends. I am so happy when she says they want to get married, which they do in the winter of 1939.

1939 brings new worries. The first German plane flies past on the 1st of September and bombs start falling over Poland. Men and boys are enlisted for the army... people are getting anxious... there are rumors... we are fearful that something momentous is happening. Germans shoot from the sky. A cart full of cabbages by the railway line is mistaken for people...

The Polish army is completely disorganized and we hear they don't have many weapons. It is as if the generals don't believe that war can happen here. When Russians arrive in tanks as big as houses, they take charge of Zloczow. At the same time, many Jews arrive from the west, believing that they might be safer from the Germans here than in their own town. Zloczow is chaotic.

Some Russians do bizarre things. One day, a group takes a whole lot of coffins onto the street. These soldiers ask some Ukrainians, neighbors of mine, to point out anyone who might be Jewish, and one of my brothers-in-law is identified as a Jew. The Jews are accosted, and thrown into the coffins, and the lids are nailed down. Soldiers and Ukrainian hooligans alike run around with the coffins, laughing and joking. They toss the coffins into the air before dropping them and running off. Who are crazier: the Russians, or the Ukrainians?

Eventually, when all is quiet, people cautiously come out of their apartments to investigate. The innocent people are released, but the experience is so horrific that there are many casualties. Soon after this, my brother-in-law dies of a heart attack.

There are Russian soldiers who behave like wild schoolboys on an adventure. For some it is their first time away from home and school and many are clumsy and uneducated, but I meet some who are kind. A young officer asks if he can live with me until he is moved on. I know I can't refuse and really, it isn't too much of a problem for a few weeks. All the same I am surprised that he has had such an unsophisticated life that he doesn't even want to use a bathroom, just a bowl of water for washing.

On July 2, 1941, 22 months after the first German planes fly over, their troops arrive on the ground in Zloczow. Panic sets in, yet, for some reason, I still don't believe anything bad will happen to me. What would they want from a woman like me? It is Tusia and Leon who must hide, and I must act normally – cooking, cleaning, as if waiting for my loved ones to come home from work.

But then German soldiers barge into my apartment looking for Jews and I babble in Polish, praying that they can't understand.

No one has ever hit me before, let alone wounded me. Blood spurts from my arm... a soldier drags me...

With many of my Jewish neighbors, I am forced to walk to Subiewski Castle – the jail where Tusia played in the garden as a young child. Those who stumble are hit on the back of the head. Anyone who slips to the ground is shot. We are crammed into the jail, men to one side, women and children to the other, locked in for the night.

The next day, with guns at our heads we are led out, forced to remove our valuables and ordered to place them in a pile by a large hole that is being dug. *Schnell, schnell*, the diggers are urged. I recognize some of them – theirs are the most anguished faces I have ever seen.

I am pushed into the pit... a volley of shots... another... and another... a bullet bites my leg... I slide to the ground feeling faint.

My memories are all I have left. I am so grateful to have Tusia as my daughter and I pray, please God, that she and Leon are alive and safe, and will escape this horror.

As if it was yesterday, I see my darling little one running towards me and I stretch out my arms to catch my bundle of joy. Tushinka...! She holds a tiny bouquet of the first spring flowers – violets and lily of the valley. I can feel my small child thrusting the flowers at me, throwing herself into my arms, showering me with moist kisses and saying, 'Happy birthday Mama'. I feel so much love for her. If only Marek had been with me to share this joy. If only he hadn't been in the army.

Violets and lily of the valley shower down... I hold out my arms again as flowers seem to fall on me... sitting among so many bodies... my arms drop... sand slips between my fingers... I stare into nothing... I no longer see... I barely breathe...

17

ON THE RUN

Zloczow 1941

When Russian troops roll into Zloczow in huge brown tanks that look as though they are made of folded cardboard, Martusia is not very worried. She is happily married to Leon, a wonderful man, which makes everything less of a problem. Life continues more or less normally, if rather crowded.

One day Yanek, a Ukrainian neighbor who works as a postman, comes to ask her a favor. He hasn't had much education and needs someone to help him fill in a legal document so he can keep a property he inherited. Martusia has worked for a lawyer after she left school so she knows what to do and doesn't mind helping. She thinks nothing more of it.

When German soldiers arrive in July, everything changes. Their invasion is much less benign and Martusia's blood freezes whenever she hears the rhythmic stomping of their boots, often accompanied by syncopated gunshots. It is a terrifying time as lives are turned upside down and inside out with soldiers barging into their homes, taking people away, killing many of them. No family is left untouched.

By some miracle Martusia escapes this terror. Not so her beautiful, loving mother, nor her wonderful, loving husband – they are taken away and killed within days of the Germans' arrival. The loss of those who matter most to her is the worst thing imaginable, so terrible that she can barely think or feel anything. But there is no time to grieve, no time to sit *shiva* mourning, no weeping or giving in to the terrible sadness. Their memories need to be preserved but first she has to find a way to stay alive, from moment to moment, day to day.

One thing she knows – she must get a German *Kennkarte,* an identity document with a photo and fingerprint. It costs quite a lot of money because, she assumes, the forged documents would require some skill.

She finds someone who says he can help her. Tamas is a strange, very restless man. He has four young children and a sick wife, so he takes a lot of risks in order to feed his family. He is short and bald except for a few hairs sticking out like pins in a cushion, and he has a big nose, flapping ears like a pig's and a twitching eye. He insists on pinching her breasts before doing the papers, saying, "Ach, how tasty!" Pfe! Why can't he keep his hands to himself? She squirms and tries to make a joke of it, knowing that she has to do whatever it takes to get that *Kennkarte*. Now she understands the gossip that he provides documents mainly for women.

A couple of days after she gets her document, a neighbor reports that Tamas was stopped by the police who have obviously been watching him. It seems a trivial matter – he was found carrying a bag of sugar and accused of stealing it. The police have taken him in for questioning and Martusia can't help wondering and worrying whether they tortured him to reveal how come he had money for sugar. Did he reveal the names of everyone for whom he had provided *Kennkarten*? People in her building talk about what might have happened to him and offer sympathy to his poor wife and children. Martusia feels uneasy about his disappearance.

The following day she meets the mother of a good friend. "Oy Martusia, what can I tell you? My Rosa was taken away for questioning this morning and I can't understand why! My lovely good daughter who never hurt anyone – what do they need her for? I'm so afraid I will never see her again. It's the worst thing that can happen to a mother, not to know! I want to die! They should have taken me, not someone with a life in front of her!"

Martusia guesses what might have happened. Rosa has probably bought a false document from Tamas as well. Maybe he keeps a list with their names. The butterflies in her stomach turn somersaults. How can she reassure Rosa's mother when she is terrified that someone could be looking for her too. She knows she can't wait to find out. Clutching her precious document and little else, she leaves Zloczow immediately, getting away before curfew.

She finds temporary refuge in a village outside Zloczow. But that haven is short-lived when some of the villagers decide that, despite her blond hair and blue eyes, Martusia must be Jewish. Why else would she be there? Her presence makes it unsafe for everyone. In desperation she walks back into town, not really knowing what to do.

And there on the street is Yanek, the Ukrainian she once helped to write the contract for his property, now wearing police uniform. He sees her and rushes over to talk. "Madam, I haven't seen you for a long time. Are you alright? Why do you look so sad and so frightened?"

It's someone a bit familiar and she breaks down as she tells him how her mother and then her husband were taken away. "They've been killed, and now I'm alone and really afraid to go back home."

"Listen," he says, "I owe you a favor. My place which you saved for us is a little bit out of town, but I am in the police force now and sometimes stay in Zloczow in my old apartment. If you like you can stay at my apartment. My wife moves between the two places so I will tell her about you. Come, it will be safe."

She doesn't have a better idea.

"The most important thing is that no one must know that you are here. I don't think anyone has seen you come in with me. You have to stay quietly under this eiderdown all day so that the neighbors won't hear or see you. Otherwise, they will report you and me. Here is a chamber pot."

So, in the heat of summer, she spends the day quietly as instructed, mostly spread-eagled under that hot feather eiderdown, trying to create an airspace that might cool her a bit. For the whole day it's as if living has left her – not eating, not passing water, nothing, just breathing in the rancid odors of the bed. Listening... remembering... waiting... for what?

For several days Yanek arrives in the evening, bringing some food. It's her cue to creep out from hiding. Before he leaves, he whispers about the killings going on in the streets, no doubt to remind her how lucky she is. When someone comes in during the afternoon and leaves her food, Martusia remains motionless in case it's somebody snooping. It turns out it was Yanek's wife leaving the food. All the same she starts to wonder how long this arrangement can last. She soon finds out.

After about a week, when Yanek comes in, she recognizes his footsteps. It has been a very hot day, and before she can move, he has come in quietly and lifted the eiderdown to let her know it will soon be night time. He finds her, her face scarlet and perspiration pouring down her back as usual. She is desperate for some water and cool air and sits up. With barely a greeting, Yanek throws her onto her back, climbs on top of her and starts to press himself against her. She is caught off guard. There is nothing appealing about this man in his grimy police uniform.

"What do you want from me? Get off me! I can't. Please! No, no! Please don't!" she whispers as she wrestles with him.

She is choking and feeling desperate as he tries to muzzle her. He is so big and much stronger than her, so she has no chance as he tugs at her clammy clothes, tearing her dress before he drags down his trousers. He enters her forcibly and she screeches in pain, like an animal that has been kicked. In response he slaps her face. Too late she remembers the neighbors. They would know that Yanek's wife isn't here. She often hears them talking, just as they must have heard her scream.

Furiously Yanek re-arranges his clothes and mutters, "For goodness' sake, shut up you stupid cow!" before leaving and taking the food with him.

The neighbors, no doubt, will be quick to tell patrolling police that they heard voices when Yanek was supposed to be alone in the apartment. Martusia can hear their voices as she slips away into the early evening shadows, carrying her shoes, looking for a hiding place. Better to risk being seen than wait to be captured.

There is still her apartment in another part of town. It won't be very safe but it's all she can think of. Luckily, she doesn't meet anyone she knows and she arrives just before curfew, sobbing and breathing heavily. She washes herself and tries to regain some composure.

About an hour later there is a knock at the door – a Polish neighbor from upstairs, who has recently joined the ever-expanding police force, comes to warn her that she's in grave danger. It reminds her how quickly everyone knows what's going on. She has to find work, and go somewhere where she won't be conspicuous.

She thinks that maybe the *Judenrat* [Jewish Council] might be able to find work for her. Otherwise, she could be taken away. The Germans must know that Jews have lived in her apartment as the *mezuzah*, or even holes on the door frame like next door, become tell-tale signs. The other Jews in the building have all been taken to the ghetto, according to the neighbor, and large numbers of them are being removed from the ghetto in trucks. Word is, every few days, many Jews are taken to a camp somewhere. She can't bear to think what will happen to them.

So here she is, early in the morning, on the run again, this time to the *Judenrat.* She knows that getting help is like a lottery. The *Judenrat* have been accepting valuables as bribes for soldiers in order to save lives, but they never know whether they will be double-crossed. Those soldiers are just as likely to take everything for themselves, then kill the people they say they are saving. Still, it's her only chance, even with her false papers.

After Leon was killed and Mundek, her father-in-law was ill with hepatitis and pneumonia, she had been the one who had cared for him, day and night. What else could she do? He was family – who else was left? But it was the *Judenrat* who benefited from his wealth. And as likely as not, the corrupt soldiers.

"You know, Martusia, I am dying," he told her. "I have talked to the *Judenrat* and told them where my valuables are hidden, where they are buried. No one can take such things to their grave".

Under the circumstances, given how much Papa has left to them,

Martusia thinks that it's not such a big favor for the *Judenrat* to help her. The spokesman tells her and six other young women that they must wear an armband sporting a yellow Star of David. What for, she wonders? She can't understand why when she could pass as non-Jewish, but she does as she is told, and the women are sent ten kilometers out of town. Stuffed together like sardines, they travel on the tray of a rough horse-drawn cart, to a farm run by Otto, a *Gauleiter*, a Ukrainian political leader working for the Nazis.

When they arrive, several young women there are planting beetroot seedlings in a field. As Martusia and the new girls dismount, another group is ushered onto the cart and driven away, all of them looking terrified, some weeping. Who would know what is happening and where they are being taken.

After eating some bread and cheese for which they are grateful, all seven women are sent out to the field. One crouching worker says in a very quiet voice, "See that man, Otto?" She glances at the man with the tomato face and neck like a balloon. "Watch out for him. He has a horse whip which he uses if you so much as lift your head."

What gives a person courage at such a time? Courage, or is it stupidity? Martusia notices the man smoking when they arrive, so with great bravado she walks across to him, holding her silver cigarette holder as if she is a movie star. The beautifully engraved object given to her by her husband has come from his father's shop.

"Hello sir, I'm one of the new girls. Would you like a cigarette?" Martusia's Ukrainian is more than passable. Cigarettes are like a universal currency and she's lucky to still have some.

"You know, I appreciate intelligent workers, especially the pretty ones." Otto licks his lips, trying to slip his hand under her skirt. She wriggles away and he reaches for his whip.

"Oh no, you won't need that. Just show us exactly what to do. You'll see how we can work," she says quickly.

Surprisingly, he doesn't use the whip while she is there, although it costs her the cigarette holder, and some dignity. She learns very fast how to keep away from his groping.

It turns out that the woman who prepares food for the workers is Otto's mistress Pasha who, before the war, was a maid for Martusia's aunt. Pasha remembers her and is terribly embarrassed that the educated and talented Martusia is expected to plant beetroot and sleep in the hay barn with the other girls.

"That job is not for someone like you. Your hands are for playing the piano, not planting beetroot," she insists and goes straight to Otto, demanding that he set up a bed for Martusia in a little office so she can do office work for him. Pasha thinks she is doing Martusia a favor. If she only knew.

That night Otto, under the influence of drink, comes to Martusia's room. "Has something happened to Pasha? Is she sick?" she is quick to ask when he appears. She pushes past him out of the office and he grabs her and puts his hand over her mouth. Acting instinctively, she lifts her knee and hits his groin. Only later does she stop to think about the risk she has taken.

Otto never says a word about the incident and she keeps her head down, working hard in the office and in the field. There are other girls with whom he does as he pleases.

After a few weeks, she persuades Otto to give her a permit to go back to town. When she arrives at her empty flat, there is, of course, nothing to eat. Slowly she walks to the ghetto where she hopes to find some food, and she can't help wondering why on earth she has returned. It is probably a really stupid thing to do, but she doesn't know what is sensible anymore and what isn't. At the gate she shows her permit and looks for somewhere to buy a meal. In what passes as a restaurant, she meets a friend, so she sits with him. At the next table two men keep staring at her.

"Who are they?" she asks quietly.

"Ukrainian police. Must be off duty. I don't understand why they are not in uniform," my friend mutters as the men approach.

"Papers!" barks one.

She hands him her permit.

"Madam, why are you here? Your permit says that you work in the country."

"Yes, I got that permit to come here. See." She doesn't really know what else to tell them. How can she explain about her dead mother and her dead husband? How can she explain that she just wants to see what's going on in her home town and her apartment, and maybe see if she can somehow stay?

"All right, all right. Just tell us where you will be tonight," grumbles one.

The only address she can think of is her apartment.

In the early evening there's a knock on her door. "Police!" And in come the two Ukrainians, this time in uniform.

"Madam, we want to see your permit again," demands one. "That's fine," he says writing down her details, and leaves.

"Not fine with me," says the other. "Let me have another look!"

He steps inside the door, takes the permit and slams the door shut behind him. She jumps when she hears the thud of his revolver that he casually drops on the table.

"What have you got to eat?" he demands.

"Nothing, that's why... that's why I went to the ghetto. I wanted some food."

The conversation goes around and around as he establishes who is in the building – no caretaker or Jewish families? As far as she knows, only Buhovski, the Polish shoemaker is downstairs, and a policeman upstairs.

Buhovski nearly dies of fright when they knock on his door. The policeman checks his papers and demands that he, Buhovski, finds him something to eat. Without waiting, they return to her apartment. The shoemaker soon arrives, trembling with fear, holding out some dry black bread and even drier sausage, probably his own meal. He is dismissed.

The door is slammed again and there they sit. It becomes like a game of cat and mouse as she watches the policeman chew with his mouth open, loudly, and he stares at her with a grin that wraps around the food. Eventually he lights a cigarette and sips something from a hip flask as he makes small talk. Conversation fades, and Martusia becomes more and more uneasy.

Casually he takes off his boots and starts to unbuckle his belt. "Get undressed!" he demands with a look that she find all too recognizable. And so unwelcome. Slowly she obeys. She is wearing just underpants when he demands, "Take that off. Dance for me."

She feels ridiculous but knows that she has to do something, so she grabs her dress and flicks it like a shawl as she spins in front of him. He sprawls on a chair, his trousers crumpled at his feet, and he starts to tap the revolver, saying, "Faster, faster! To my rhythm!"

After a few minutes she is so giddy that she slows down and wobbles to a chair, clutching at her dress.

"You need a drink!" he insists, pushing his flask towards her. "And you don't need that," as he snatches her dress and throws it onto the floor. He opens his cigarette case and stares at the emptiness.

"Do you have any cigarettes?"

"I'm sorry, I don't have any."

"Then get dressed and go and get some. No, you don't need your coat or your shoes," he laughs. "Ask Buhovski," he says, dragging his trousers back up.

He unlocks the door and she rushes to Buhovski's apartment to beg for cigarettes. But he too has none. "Tuberculosis," he explains, pointing to his chest. "Me and my wife."

"Then come and tell the policeman, please, or he will come and shoot us both!"

Buhovski stands at the door of her apartment, gabbling incoherently, shuffling from one foot to the other, eyes focused on his boots.

"Go and get me cigarettes," orders the policeman.

"But sir, it's after curfew. How can I?"

"No," says my captor. "Already? I have to go!" He fastens his trousers and grabs his belt, while flinging on his jacket, remembering to pick up the menacing revolver before rushing out, calling, "I'll be back later."

Buhovski slips back to his apartment.

Do come, she thinks, but don't expect to find anyone here.

There is no sleep for her and at first light she starts the long walk back to the farm.

When she gets there she hears Pasha: "You girls will have to go! Now! Quickly! The Germans are coming. Maybe tomorrow they will be..."

Martusia is terrified that she will be deported to a concentration camp but she agrees with Pasha that it's best that they wait until it is almost dark. Meanwhile the girls rehearse over and over what to do. What if they are raped, injured, killed … left lying in the forest? They agree to split up.

Martusia has her false papers and a few coins, and for once she is not totally alone. Together with another girl, she manages to get on a train to Lvov where they part company. Using a contact provided by the *Judenrat,* she reaches Genowefa and Henryk Seidel, a kind couple who send her to their daughter Janina and her husband Roman Bochenski in Kolonia Krzywczycka 76 on the outskirts of the city. At last she can draw breath.

18

A STORY TO BE TOLD, AGAIN

Zloczow 1941

Martusia and Leon have been happily married for almost six months when she applies for a job as a secretary to work for the Russians. The Russians have occupied Poland for the past two years and she is working in one of the warehouses from which supplies are distributed to soldiers. She speaks Ukrainian reasonably well; it's near enough to Russian. Displaying her usual *chutzpa*, she insists that she can manage. It doesn't worry her that she has never used a Russian typewriter before. The manager tests her and the copy she produces is full of what look like black spiders where she has typed over and over, but as she guesses, they don't have anyone else to do the job.

Leon has a German engineering degree from the time he spent in Czechoslovakia and he's been given an important job at the local electro-station. His father is so proud, as is Martusia. With both jobs they earn enough money to help her mother.

It's a really dangerous time for everyone in Zloczow. The talk is that Russians arrest people who they identify as capitalists. Actually, from what Martusia can tell, they arrest people for any little mistake they can fabricate. Her mother Zanetta isn't very worried. She lives in an attractive apartment and is able to make any environment look good. The apartment is stylishly furnished and creatively arranged with everything she owns, including furnishings she has created herself, so she believes that Russians looking for capitalists will have to look elsewhere.

Leon's father, Mundek, on the other hand, has been a banker. What's more he has inherited several properties from his family so Leon worries a lot about him. Mundek owns the apartment building where Leon and Martusia live, as well as owning another building not too far away where he lives with his younger son. And there are several buildings outside the township that he owns. Downstairs, in the building where Mundek lives, is an apartment for Mundek's father-in-law who has recently married a very pretty, extremely young woman.

The talk has been that the Germans are advancing, and out in the streets there is a sense of terror at the thought of what might happen. Meanwhile people are dragged from their homes in the dead of night and no one knows where the Russian soldiers are taking them. The suspicion is that some are sent to Siberia. Leon worries that his father and brother are vulnerable and could be taken so, having no better idea of how to help, he and Martusia decide that they should both move in with them. She can't help wondering what on earth they could do to protect anyone, and judging by what is going on, their jobs won't even help.

There are food shortages but they manage and Martusia feels lucky that they aren't suffering, apart from nagging anxiety. After work she and Leon go straight to her mother's apartment, as does Mundek, while Leon's younger brother decides to go to his friend's home. Zanetta cooks for them all and as soon as dinner is over, they all rush away to get back to their apartment before curfew. Zanetta loves having them come to her and it is especially good for Mundek who has been a widower since Leon was 15.

Martusia has a sense that the Russians are perpetually suspicious, always checking on everyone, so she and Leon agree they have to be careful. But they aren't really sure what to be careful about as the situation changes every day. All the same, nothing bothers her too much as she and Leon are so very much in love. It is all they can do not to embarrass the family with their desire for each other.

July 3, 1941 is imprinted in Martusia's memory. The day is thick with black clouds and deafening thunder. The maid, Dusia, who had been with Zanetta since Martusia was a very young child, had left a few weeks earlier to marry her boyfriend, to go to live in the mountains. On this particular day she has rushed back to Zanetta's apartment, bringing drab inconspicuous skirts and scarves. Breathlessly she pants, "*Proszę pani* [please madam], you and the young madam, must put on these clothes. Like Polish peasants. Please. You need to come with me now because they are killing Jews out there. Maybe we can save you at my home in the mountains."

"What do you mean they are killing Jews?" demands Zanetta. "They are not looking for me. I didn't do anything wrong."

"I know, but it's the German army that is coming this way and they are killing people. Anyone. Everyone. They have gone mad!"

'No," says Zanetta. "Why should I run? Thank you, Dusia, but I will stay."

That beautiful brave Zanetta, that generous little woman with a giant heart keeps cooking as if nothing is happening. When Martusia and Leon rush in after work with Mundek not far behind, they are trying to get off the street as quickly as possible. Zanetta calmly reports what her maid said, then directs them to where they should all hide.

"There is no need for me to hide, what for do they have to kill me?"

"Please Mamushka, please hide with us," implores Martusia, but her mother shakes her head and keeps preparing food.

In Zanetta's bedroom there is a cupboard placed diagonally across a corner, and Mundek squeezes into the triangular space behind it. Leon urges his father to curl up as small as he can, but Mundek's legs seem to have lost their ability to bend. Martusia prays no one will see him.

The balcony is like another room outside the bedroom and in the wall separating the apartment from the one next door, there is an unusual alcove that seems to be the result of a miscalculation during building. Zanetta doesn't like how untidy it looks so has hung a richly patterned Persian carpet over it. In front of the carpet is a dressing table with a mirror and a few precious ornaments.

Mundek owns a jewelry shop downstairs in the building. He has removed all the valuables from their boxes and has stored his treasure trove deep in the ground at a nearby property. The only other person who knows the location is Leon. At Zanetta's suggestion, Mundek has stored his mountain of empty boxes in the alcove on the balcony. But now they are in the way, so Martusia and Leon push the boxes out of the space and huddle together in the empty alcove. Outside there are sounds of frequent shooting and screaming, accompanied by the ominous clatter of an unseasonal storm. The sound of screams of fear is getting closer by the minute.

Suddenly heavy footsteps fill the room, followed by loud staccato orders in German. Martusia is gripped with fear when she hears her mother's trembling voice call out in rapid Polish, "Stay where you are!", the last words Martusia ever hears her mother say, words that echo long after the footsteps move away, long after the thumps and her mother's screams of pain.

For several hours they sit, anguish and terror turning them to stone. Eventually Martusia, desperate to go to the toilet, so she cautiously moves out of hiding. Taking off her shoes, she slips across the room quietly, bringing back the chamber pot, first for Mundek, then for Leon. Stupidly she looks for her mother, for a sign. Anything. There is a smear of blood on the kitchen floor and another on the carpet by the door. She who bled so easily and complained so little. What have they done to her? Where have they taken her?

The night is coal black. An unexpected dagger of wind flies through a bullet hole in the window frame. It doesn't feel like summer. Martusia hears voices in the street and shrinks in fear. Gray-green pellets, the peas that Zanetta had been cooking, are in a saucepan where she left them. She passes them around and they devour them, silently, fearfully.

"We must stay hidden," she whispers as she returns to her hiding place. The shooting in the street continues. Who is in the firing line? Please, please let it not be her mother.

All night and the next day they stay in hiding, afraid that floorboards might creak and give them away. Someone might come in and see them. Martusia's legs ache. She has pins and needles in her feet from being in the same position for so long and dust from the hanging carpet fills her throat. The silence in the apartment is oppressive, thick with unspoken questions. But nothing will persuade them to go anywhere. Occasionally she dozes a little, comforted by the embrace of her husband, but she keeps jerking awake, terrified by any noise.

During the second afternoon they hear people crashing around next door. It sounds as though somebody is searching for something, maybe valuables. The locked door that separates the neighboring dentist's rooms from Zanetta's apartment is smashed down. Then clomping footsteps again. Closer. Someone is rifling through the discarded jewelry boxes. Martusia shrinks into a small ball and winces as she hears some of her mother's crystal and crockery being reduced to splinters.

Then a triumphant shout. The intruders have glimpsed a leg. Four German soldiers drag Mundek out of his hiding place, one of them bellowing, "Where is everything from these boxes?"

"There is nothing," he whimpers. "I used to have a shop downstairs but it's all gone."

"What are these?" they ask, pulling out a watch and some small treasures from his pockets, along with Leon's engineering degree and physics book, which for some strange reason Mundek always carries with him. Pride manifests itself in strange ways, and Martusia wonders if it is possible this might help them. Can Mundek keep calm and not give them away? Or are they all doomed?

"They... they are my son's," Mundek stammers in German.

"And where is he?"

"I... I don't know. Not here. He... went."

"Ach so he studied at a German university in Czechoslovakia." A pause. "All right, we will leave you here with this note. Here."

The ridiculous piece of paper says: "This Jew has to be left alone" – as if that will help anyone.

"They've gone," Mundek says after what seems like an eternity.

"You can come out." He is pale and trembling. Leon holds his father close for a few minutes and Mundek tells them about the diamond that has miraculously appeared from his shoe. The soldiers took it and whatever unbroken valuables they could before stomping out of the apartment.

In a daze Martusia goes to the kitchen and starts to cook whatever she can put together quickly – carrots, a potato, two eggs. They are ravenous and devour the food at speed. Whenever they hear voices in the hallway they rush back into hiding.

Another long day passes and the next time she steps out to cook Martusia is more cautious about what she prepares. The smell of scrambled eggs from the day before has lingered for a dangerously long time. Strangers come – they are speaking Polish – and they hear the intruders helping themselves to the furniture. They make two visits and leave very little behind.

Finally, the shooting outside subsides and Martusia musters enough courage to step out of the apartment to go down into the street, where she encounters a friendly Polish neighbor.

"My mother... they took her away. All I can hear in my head are her last words." She sobs for the first time since the nightmare began.

"You know," the neighbor says, "the Germans didn't come to us at the back of the building. Maybe they didn't realize there was another apartment there. Come with me and I will hide you all in the basement."

"Please don't cry, darling," whispers Leon, stroking Martusia as they lie in the basement on a narrow bench covered with thin cushions. Leon's touch is soothing but she can't stop weeping. A pile of coal separates them from others hiding in the cellar and drunken German singing in the courtyard above them drowns out Leon's gentle voice.

"Listen, my darling Tusia. Please, stop crying. Listen. You don't look Jewish so you should try to save your life. I doubt that I can, but you might."

"You are talking such nonsense," she whimpers.

"Please, Tusia. Please stop. I love you so much and can't bear to see you so upset. Listen, I have to tell you where my father has hidden some jewelry, something that might save you."

He wraps his arms around her, pulling her close, caressing her, stroking her with his gentle fingers covering her face with kisses. Then he whispers directions. Despite her fear, she feels safe in his arms and eventually falls asleep.

That night she dreams she is digging the ground with a teaspoon and her bare hands. Drunken German soldiers circle around her and close in, holding back just long enough for her to unearth Mundek's treasure trove. She wakes with a start.

In the morning Leon reminds her of the pregnant cat they left in his father's apartment.

"Tusia, maybe you could look at what's happening. The cat must be dying of hunger and she must have had her kittens by now. Please go, sweetheart. I can't imagine anyone will stop you."

Leon and his father join three others in a nearby cellar. As she leaves, Martusia hears the caretaker urging the men who are arguing about which cellar is safest, to keep their voices down.

A Polish friend greets her in the street and Martusia tells her about her mother, how desperate she is to find her.

"I am so sorry to tell you what I've heard," the woman says. "For two days and nights German soldiers took a lot of people to Sobiewski Castle, you know, the old jail, the *Zamec*. I heard that a bunch of Ukrainian hooligans went with them and they were all shooting like crazy. People are saying maybe 1,500 people were killed the second night after they were taken. Who knows how many there were? Such a shocking thing to happen! Why? Why?"

Martusia doesn't have time to fully process this information because her father-in-law's apartment building is swarming with German soldiers. The apartment has been stripped bare – carpet, furniture, everything has gone.

"Who are you?" asks a young officer.

"I... I live here but I went to see my mother. Why are there no beds, no carpets, nothing?" she responds in German.

"We found it like this. Our garrison is next door and we needed places for officers. Listen, I will send some soldiers to find out what happened to your things. Come with me."

They discover that Buhovski, the shoemaker who lives downstairs in the apartment block, feels like he has won a lottery. He even has her umbrella and underwear displayed like trophies.

"You will have everything returned when we leave," says the officer, "but tell me, why did you go away?"

"Because I was afraid. I'm..." Carelessly, she almost admits to being Jewish, but fortunately the officer is talkative and happy to interrupt. He has no orders yet, he informs her.

She sways unsteadily.

"Are you hungry?" he asks. "I can give you some bread and sausage. Some cheese. I even have an apple."

"Thank you. And then I must look for my cat."

She finds Leon's grandfather still in his apartment.

"You know, when an officer forced open Mundek's door that cat nearly tore out his eyes," he informs her with a wide smile. "I saw it myself. So did my wife, didn't you, my love?"

"Why did the Germans not come to you?"

"Oh, they came all right. There were two officers. They looked at me, and then at my beautiful wife... huh... and, well, for some strange reason they wouldn't let anybody touch us. They didn't even ask us for papers. They probably have their eyes on my wife. Maybe they think I'm her father, or her grandfather. Ha ha ha!" He grins at Martusia, then remembers their problems.

"You'd better bring Leon here. That grandson of mine will be safer with us. Oh, and by the way, your cat and her three scrawny kittens have made themselves at home here so I have the pleasure of cleaning up their mess."

She walks the two and a half blocks back to her mother's apartment, wondering how she can move her husband safely. As she approaches the apartment building, she sees German soldiers, guns at the ready, accompanied by a group of loud Ukrainian thugs forming a circle around a group of men who have their hands in the air. The men who have been hiding in our building. Including Leon and his father.

"Get away!" she hears as a gun is whacked across her chest, and she almost falls down a short flight of steps. Leon stares at her, unblinking, and she feels him willing her to stay silent. She is winded and her chest hurts, but she follows the men, at a distance, to the police station.

There is a bleak courtyard in front of the grimy stone building. Guards prevent her from entering, no matter how much she protests. She slides to the ground and sits outside the courtyard for what seems like hours, sobbing quietly, until she sees a man standing high behind a parapet, staring down at her. She is convinced it is her husband and she leaps up, ready to call out to him. Then she hears a shot and he disappears.

She wants to scream, "That's my husband. Let him go!" but the words are stuck, thundering inside her head. The guards ignore her and she waits, and waits, not knowing why, except that her legs are like lead when she finally drags herself up.

Light is fading when her father-in-law emerges and limps towards where she is standing. He looks old, has a cut over one eye and he is walking unsteadily. But nobody stops him.

"Come. It's almost curfew. Where is Leon? How did you get out?" Martusia asks quietly as she offers him her arm for him to lean on.

"I don't know where he is. I think they took him away." Mundek avoids her eyes as they walk on. "I gave them two watches. They asked if I had anything more to buy my son's freedom, but I had given them all I had."

"What do you mean? Couldn't you have given Leon one of the watches? Anything? You bought your freedom and not your son's!"

Speechless, she shrinks away from him. Mundek stands cowed, a broken man. She knows in her heart that she will never see the love of her life again. How can she forgive this man? Slowly they walk to his apartment, a meter and a life between them as they weep silently, each alone in their grief.

Melbourne 1950

For a long time Martusia had wondered if she would ever stop feeling that it was impossible to recover from losing the love of her life. It didn't seem possible to keep living. Yet a decade later, here she is, creating a new life. She is now known as Martha, and the past is as firmly behind her as possible.

It's a catch-you-in-the-throat dusty February morning and she is in a crowded bus heading for Helena's new school. The same intense dry heat had caught her by surprise almost a year earlier, when she and her husband Feliks disembarked from the Toscana with their small daughter at Port Melbourne.

She bends towards her daughter and murmurs in French that they will get off the bus soon, at which point the child flaps her mother away. To any observer, it seems as though the heat is making the child irritable, but in fact she just hates it when anyone notices her mother speaking in French. Standing near them is a man who can't stop grinning as he watches them. "People always stare," Helena will tell her mother once they are off the bus.

Martha notices the man watching them, and at a glance, she takes in his trim muscular body, his unruly dark hair and piercing blue eyes. He might be a bit younger than her she surmises. An open-necked white shirt with short sleeves, gray shorts, dark gray long socks and sandals seem an unlikely outfit for a professional man going to work. And he has a tattoo on his arm. Definitely not a professional man. A tattoo. Navy?

Navy, army, uniformed forces... guns, tanks...bodies on the ground...no, no, bad memories, need to forget...

Instinctively she flashes him the kind of look that became a self-protective habit during the war. Then she feels silly. What is she thinking?

The next day the same man stands up to offer her his seat as she moves through the jumble of people and bags. Martha mutters "thank you" and drags Helena onto her knee as the bus jerks forward over the pot-holes in North Road. The man ignores the strap that dangles from the rail and finds a rhythm, rocking from one foot to the other, as if on the waves. He watches and listens until he hears Martha speak to her daughter in French. To his amusement there is a replay of the child's scowling behavior of the previous day.

"*Bonjour madame, je parle Français. Un peu,*" he stammers. She looks up and smiles. She has begun to believe that no one in this country speaks anything other than English, which makes every day a struggle. But here is someone prepared to try. Talking to someone other than her grumpy daughter is most appealing. In fact, the man himself is appealing.

Melbourne 2003

"You know, Helen, making a movie about Mum's survival during the war, and then how she started her life again in Australia seemed such a great idea back in the 70s when I was starting to make training films. I had no idea how impossible it would be to make a film about her. She freaked out before I got going."

Eve and I are having one of our many lengthy phone conversations, trying to unravel more details of our parents' lives, things they didn't want to talk about – things we tried to unpick by stealth.

"Jenny Pausacker was the only person to have patiently sat listening and recording all those double-sided dictaphone tapes of Mum's life story. I listened to some parts and started asking Mum questions. That's when she suddenly made a huge fuss. It seemed ridiculous, but I couldn't go ahead with the film. So I phoned Jenny to tell her the project wasn't happening and I packed away the tapes."

"That must have been so disappointing. What do you think tripped her up?"

"I can only guess. Do you remember those tapes? I probably didn't show them to you after Mum screamed at me that they weren't true. I'll never forget her anger.

“’No, no, no! What did that Jenny tell you? It’s all wrong Evinka,’ she insisted.

“I did try to explain that she must have said something... after all, Jenny taped her. But she just went on and on: ‘Tape, shmape! It’s not true! It wasn’t happening like that! Jenny is mixing me up with somebody else.’

“I just couldn’t argue with her. But now... maybe so many years after she died, I can try again.”

“Wow, I never knew the whole story. Send me the tapes and I’ll transcribe them. They might give me some clues about the strange things emerging in my artwork. I’ve been making notes to try to explain the Holocaust references in what I’m creating, and the notes seem to expand into sentences and paragraphs. Maybe there’s more to come for both of us.”

All three of my girls left home when they were quite young and have gone out into the world. I’ve always missed them terribly, welcoming the times we are together. But there is more time for work, and projects like transcribing Mum’s tapes. It’s a real labor of love, in some ways not unlike my absorbing stitched art projects. Both consume me and I often forget how late it is.

Just listening to Mum’s voice on tape, her unique phrasing and pronunciation of her thoughts in English, takes me back to those years when she and I would both work late into the night. The best times were in the early hours of the morning when I was an architecture student. Mum would emerge from cutting and glueing tiny tiles on her latest mosaic project, and I would be trying to meet my deadline for yet another architectural assignment. We would sometimes sit in the kitchen, talking over a cup of tea about all the things that mattered. On one occasion at three o’clock in the morning Dad stumbled in to find out what all the laughter was about. Seeing us joking and looking so happy, he decided he needed a cup of tea too. Such good memories.

I’ve been transcribing the tapes for a while. It’s a really nice way to do it, sitting in my studio in the back garden where large pohutukawa trees and an oak embrace the small building. It was Mum who convinced me I needed a studio for my work. She didn’t think it was a good idea for my artwork to take up all available surfaces in the house, which she considered quite small. She was absolutely right when she told me that the children needed to eat at the dining room table, not in front of TV, and the table shouldn't be my work bench. On top of which, the little business I had for eight years, seemed to invade every room of the house. The business, promoting and distributing my sister's educational and business management programs soon migrated to the studio as well.

One painful story Mum told us was about when the Germans came to their apartment. With hindsight now that I'm trying to pick over every word of her tapes, I realize that what is now being revealed is not the same as I remember. We had grown up believing that Mum had been in the basement looking for a kitten when her mother called out, "Stay where you are." We accepted this version because it was something to hang onto, something we thought we really knew. A little bit of testimony. But really, given that her mother's apartment was on the first floor, how could she have heard her mother call out if she was two floors down?

I phoned Eve to talk to her about it.

"Yeah, memory can work that way. Abbreviating a story, then embroidering it – it's how mythology develops. Including Mum's story."

"All the same, Eve, it felt a bit like someone had trampled on a little scrap of our history. I felt manipulated, even so long after she died."

"Yeah, I understand. We just have to live with two versions.

"By the way, while you were uncovering all those details, what else did you discover? I know you think it's crazy, but I still can't get past the idea that you and I come from different gene pools. Maybe it's stupid, but while we're uncovering more about Mum's real life, let's get that test done. Come on, Helen, DNA tests are heaps easier and getting better all the time."

I'm not going to argue with Eve. Perhaps there is more for us to discover. I've known for ages that Eve needs to get this idea of different fathers out of her system once and for all, so maybe we'll do the DNA test soon.

It's becoming more obvious that Mum might have never fully revealed her past to the researcher. I slouch back and stare out through the rain-spattered window and watch the silhouetted cabbage trees swaying as they reach for the dark gray sky. But what I can see, as though it's happening right in front of me, is Dad all those years ago, on one of his visits to New Zealand. He's throwing a ball to my little girls, laughing about his butter fingers and telling them how he played soccer when he was a boy. He is being such a loving grandfather. Strangely, I can't remember him ever throwing a ball to me. Nor to Eve. But that doesn't prove anything. I know he loved us as much as he adored his grandchildren.

Eve sends me a text: "By the way, please email me your transcript so far. Now I'm really curious to know what's in it."

It's late and I'm wide awake. I email the transcript to Eve and wonder if she will find anything I have missed.

Weeks later Eve forwards an email from a stranger saying her parents Dixie and Gloria Lee were friends with our parents. She reckons she and Eve are sisters. They meet and Eve sends me a photo of the two of them. She phones urging me to check my emails.

I stare at the photo and call her back. 'How freaky! Who the hell is your doppelganger? She looks a lot like you."

"I told you Dixie had to be my father. I think I've just known it for years. Well, I've known it in my gut. So Helen, we finally need to do some tests. Okay if I send you a DNA pack? Micheline – Mish, who's Dixie's youngest kid will take one too."

This time I can't find any reason to object. "Sure. Send me the pack."

"You know I'm remembering that he was the family friend who never really fitted in with any of the European Jewish friends – all those people who spoke Polish and Russian and German. He didn't fit with Mum's artist friends either? A loner..."

We laugh.

"Yeah, he was a bit of a fish out of water in any of those groups.

Still, I've always had this strange familiar feeling about him and I've never understood how come we got to know him so well. Don't you remember how he used to hang around when Dad was at work?"

"Yeah. And then there was that time he and his wife looked after us when Mum and Dad went overseas, which seemed weird."

"Well, a while back I had come across one of Dixie's sons and I had thought that the two of us might go for some DNA tests. He agreed at first but the tests didn't happen because he wouldn't sit in my car – because it had leather seats and he was a vegan."

"That's funny."

"Later he told his sister about me. Her curiosity got the better of her so she looked me up on the internet, saw photos of me, and... well, you know the rest."

Within three weeks the results are back.

"You're going to be amazed, Helen. Listen to this – it's 99.99% positive that Mish and I share a parent. But wait, here's the kicker – for you and me, there's just 79.66% certainty we are sisters."

Eve decides to get in touch with Dixie but doesn't have the courage to knock on his door. My oldest daughter Melina has come to Werribee with her and it's the first time she has seen her aunt totally lose her composure. Eve pulls over to side of the road, trembling, so Melina phones him from Eve's car, introducing herself. She reminds him she is Martha's oldest granddaughter and tells him she is doing research about her beloved grandmother. When she suggests they meet, he agrees.

So there they all are at the mall – Dixie, Mem – his wife of 30 years - and Melina and Eve. And from the time they were in the car, Melina and Eve just keep filming. The evidence, haha, and the reason I have such a clear picture of what happened.

Dixie is pretty cagey at first, and doesn't say much. After his surprise, he seems genuinely pleased to see Eve after so many years. They start talking about how many kids Eve has, and she tells him about Kim and Ben. She laughingly asks him about his family. For a moment he can't look her in the eye, and says something about too many kids to keep track of. Mem looks on quizzically. He says it's nine, but Eve knows after talking to Mish that it's ten kids, although two are not his biological children. And four marriages. And some lovers. This is too crazy but Eve knows it to be true.

She asks him when he had met Martha and he confidently says 1949, a few months after we had arrived in Melbourne.

"Did you meet on a bus?" Eve asks, to which he proudly replies, "Yes."

"The North Road bus?"

'Haha, yes."

They talk for some time – about his surveying, the streets named after Martha and Eve, his family... until eventually Eve says, "What about me? You know that I'm your kid."

He laughs like he's always done, not quite denying it. They both know it's true. And yes, he eventually does admit it.

By this time a security guard in the mall tells Eve to stop filming.

Back in the car, Eve phones to tell me. Melina says that now they know everyone is half-related, they will just have to love each other twice as much to make up for it.

Not for the first time I start to wonder about memory and how it can trick us. For someone in his very senior years, Dixie has a really good memory. He is sure he met our mother in 1949. I know that I started at Kilvington Girls' Grammar School in 1950, turning five that year, and I was there on that bus with Mum and Dixie when they met.

On Mum's tape, she recalls meeting a man on the bus and he spoke a bit of French. She states that she was pregnant with Eve at the time. Was she covering her tracks? It is a small detail, yet once again there appears to be more than one version of the story.

Eve and I are on the phone again the next day.

"Hey Helen, got a few minutes?"

"How are you, my half-sister?"

"To be honest, I'm really not sure. I probably didn't expect to find a parent alive. Not to mention suddenly having a whole lot of siblings. It's overwhelming but I'm okay."

"And do you feel ever so slightly guilty that you've discovered Mum's biggest secret that she always said she would take to her grave?"

"Hm... I suppose, in a way, but I don't feel guilty because it means I now know who I am. What I'm trying to come to terms with is that the father who I adored, and who adored me, wasn't actually my biological father. Which means that my grandchildren aren't his great grandchildren. Well, he'll always be my real father. He was the man who brought me up. I'll always be Feliks and Martha's daughter. "But then there's Dixie – almost a stranger, and he's linked biologically to me. I guess I'm prepared to get to know him better. It sounds like he's had a pretty insane kind of life.

"How about you, Helen? What do you think about it all?"

"I'm feeling surprisingly fine about it. That's probably to be expected. You've psyched me up for this for so many years when you were just going by a gut feeling. In fact, I'm smiling, thinking how accurate you were. I will never criticize or judge you again for following your intuition."

"Well, we knew what Mum was like. And I was right!"

"For me it's like a puzzle piece falling into place, especially when I remember some curious things from my childhood which are starting to make sense. You and I just need to keep talking about it until it really sinks in."

A week later: "Hi Helen, how are you getting on with our new reality?"

"Like you shattering the nuclear family story and having a multi-generational Aussie heritage as well as an Eastern European one? And a Holocaust one at that. It's a bit weird but I've got used to the idea, although I still find it hard to believe that Mum could have had an affair for 15 years, and managed to keep it secret. She must have told at least one of her friends. And they must have been so loyal. Honestly Eve, what a secret to live with!"

"Mum used to say she wished she'd had the pill like we did. Remember? Now we know why. Dixie's been telling me stuff – so matter-of-fact – like how they would have conceived me on a beach behind a boatshed. It's hardly surprising that she got pregnant with all the sex they had. And they would go to the Dandenongs for picnics."

“Did it ever occur to us to ask why she was so familiar with the place.”

“He says they made no demands of each other. He told her she was beautiful and she lapped it up. Well, that’s my interpretation.”

“But don’t you remember Dad saying that sort of thing to her? Telling her she was beautiful?”

“Oh yeah, he was pretty affectionate and loving towards her, and both men obviously knew she craved it. But I guess her relationship with Dixie was different.”

“And do you remember how she would joke that every woman needed a provider, a lover and a handyman?”

“Uhuh.”

“So here’s the big question – tell me Eve, who was the handyman?”

We burst out laughing.

“The bit I don’t get is how she put up with Dixie’s wild life. He was such a rogue.”

“Yeah. He’s got no shame and keeps telling me more about his past. As far as I can tell, this man, my biological father was neglectful of his kids and his four wives, except Mem. I suppose he and Mum understood that they would never share some parts of their lives”

“That’s right. What he and Mum had was as if they were in a capsule outside of their normal lives. It’s as though he didn’t interrupt the main rhythm of her life – he just slipped into the spaces around her normal routines. And she didn’t seem to care about the rest.”

I reckon their affair eventually petered out through lack of opportunity. It might have ended when Dixie built his yacht and set off with two women and a small child. That ménage á trois was possibly one thing too many for Mum to accommodate.”

“And wasn’t that about the time that Mum was diagnosed with ulcerative colitis? The war, the stresses in her life, all the pretending she needed to do for survival, the self-protection – maybe all that was taking its toll. And I’m sure she wouldn’t have stayed alive if she hadn’t done all that.”

Eve and I surprise ourselves and those around us with how easily we’ve accepted knowing about Mum’s affair. It’s not an issue for us that we are half-sisters – it hasn't changed our relationship. In fact, we're probably closer than ever and are both really happy that Mum found romance and love again in Australia after all she had lost.

All this information becomes very much part of Eve's documentary film, "Man on the Bus", and I'm happy to help. Her overseas business trips now include interviews with friends and family. Whenever I go to Melbourne, there's invariably a camera person at the ready, and a list of questions. What's more, Eve is using some footage of Mum's amateur movies which are incredibly revealing. Excerpts become part of her film which premieres late 2019. It's an unusual and really interesting way of processing our feelings.

I'm realizing how tragedy in Mum's early years, being desperate to feel secure and experience passionate love again, has shaped her life. It's the stuff of romantic movies – and she loved movies, especially the ones with good looking actors. Who can deny Mum the right to be happy after what she went through?

There is a point where I wonder how Mum would have felt about Eve making a film about our lives, especially hers. On the one hand, she would have absolutely loved being the center of attention and having a movie made about her. But on the other hand, she would have been mortified and totally outraged that we could even contemplate damaging her reputation. But then, she'll never know.

Did Feliks know? While Eve's film was being made, and even after it, this has remained an open question – asked over and over. We can only surmise. Dad's behavior towards Eve gave no hint of suspicion she wasn't his daughter. He was an adoring, kind generous father to us both – equally. And so loving to our children – Melina, Natalia, Nikki and Kim (Ben was yet to be born when he died).

I love the fact that my adorable grandson, Natalia's son, Marlow Felix Koppenhagen, has inherited Dad's sparkly laughing eyes and his arithmetical ability. And I am reminded that the same numbers gene was inherited by all three of my daughters. It seems logical that Marlow should be the recipient of my treasured geometry set given to me all those years ago by Dad's best friend Fred Stern.

Eve's movie developed a life of its own and was screened not just in Australia but much more widely. Conversations and curiosity led Eve to asking Bob Weis for Dad's testimony used in his documentary 'Proud to Live'. We listened and I transcribed. And just like that, Dad mentioned it in passing – a throw-away comment that gave us the answer.

I immediately phoned Eve, and said, "I've found it! Dad didn't know!"

"What? Oh, you mean... What makes you say that?"

"He talks proudly about us both having his genes."

"Wow! That's amazing!"

"And there's another thing, maybe a clue we missed all along, and I've only just thought about it. He named you after his sisters! It matched naming me after my grandmothers. He wouldn't have done that if there was any question about you being his child. And Mum would surely have gone along with that decision."

"You're right. I'm relieved he didn't know."

"Yeah, I'm sure he wouldn't have been able to keep a secret like Mum did – she who was adamant there were secrets she would take to her grave. But she didn't know about DNA."

PHOTOS

Hela Asz, Feliks's mother

Zanetta Wagner, Martha's mother

Marek Wagner, Martha's father

Martha c 1918

Martha and Feliks's wedding, Lvov, November 1944

Martha c 1948

Feliks, Helena, Martha in Monte Carlo 1948

Feliks and Martha Ash leaving Europe 1949

Helen, Feliks, Eve in Murrumbeena 1952

Martha, Helen, Feliks, Eve in Murrumbeena, 1952

Martha and Feliks enjoy life in Melbourne

Eve and Helen 1980s Photo: Ponch Hawkes

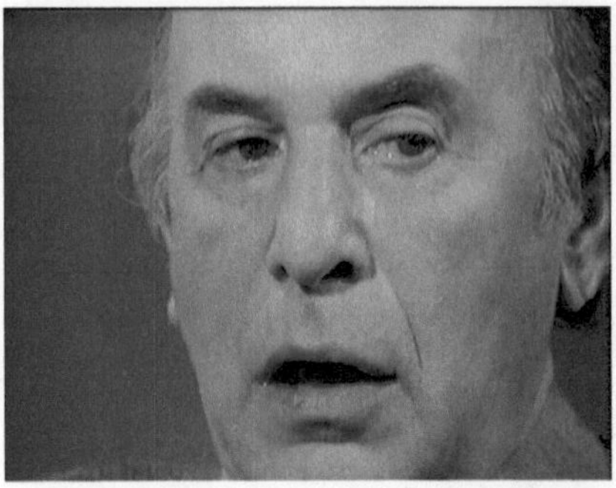

Feliks gives an interview for documentary “Proud to Live”

Sign by Janowska camp

Janowska Holocaust memorial 2009

Walking into Janowska camp – Helen, Eve, Igor (interpreter) 2009

Memorial in the Zloczow forest unveiled in 2009

Plaque remembering Jews buried at Sobiewski Castle

Janina and Roman Buchenscy risked their lives when they gave refuge to Martha

Nina Zarel who, with her husband Eddie, known as Mundek when he escaped from Janowska with Feliks, spent their modest savings to buy a pram for Martha and Feliks's baby Helena in Crakow 1945.

Anatol Kark and Helen whose lives as babies in Crakow 1946 were intertwined, meet for the first time in Auckland 2025.

Mosaic mural by Martha at Ash Manufacturing Co. Pty. Ltd. factory

"From Creation to Redemption" – mural at Temple Beth Israel, Melbourne by Martha Ash 1990

"Honouring the Memory", silk installation, from exhibition "Eighteen for Life, Ten to Remember" 2002 (Photo: Haru Sameshima)

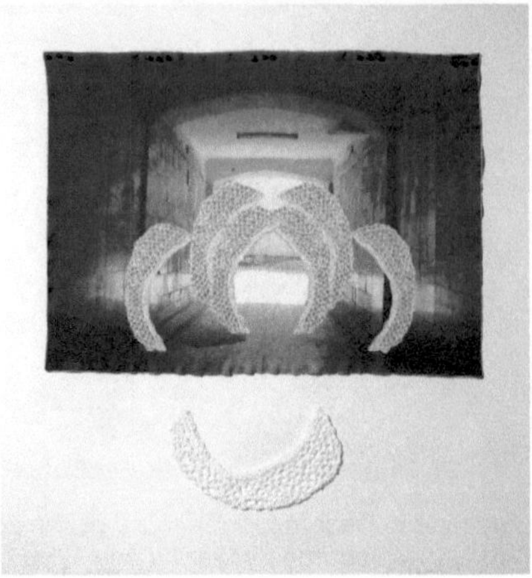

“Seeking evidence Lvov”, digital photograph on silk and crocheted cotton. From exhibition “Tracing” 2011 by Helen Schamroth (Photo: Howard Williams)

“Seeking evidence Zloczow”(digital photograph on silk and crocheted cotton), from exhibition “Tracing” 2011 by Helen Schamroth (Photo: Howard Williams)

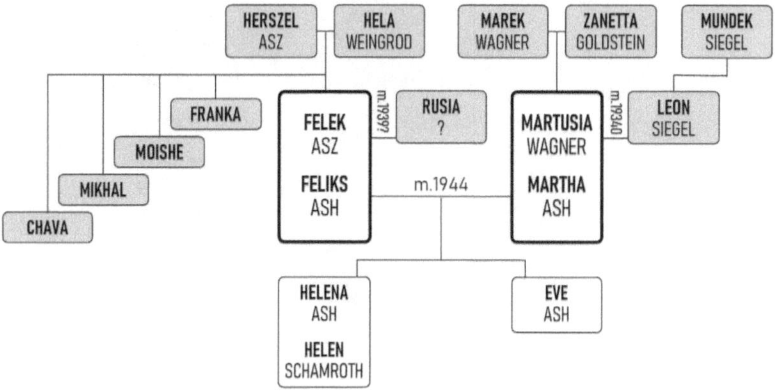

My Family Tree as I knew it in 1968

ACKNOWLEDGMENTS

This is the true story of my family – to the best of my knowledge. But writing this book did not start that way.

It began when I was creating artworks that referenced my parents' Holocaust survival. These were for my exhibition "Eighteen for Life, Ten to Remember"and I was trying to make sense of my notes, which became phrases, then paragraphs. Before long I had three fictional stories. Over a drink after an Arts Board meeting, Dame Fiona Kidman kindly offered to read them, and her advice was that I should just keep writing. I thank her for her faith in me.

With 18 fictional connected stories written, I made good use of The NZ Society of Authors Assessment Programme and Graham Lay provided supportive and helpful input. My thanks go to him and to early readers of my manuscript, John Smythe and Navina Clemerson who provided feedback and were most encouraging. The greatest gift was from my very good friend Jane Schaverien, may she rest in peace, with whom I exchanged stories, critiquing and supporting each other's efforts. She asked to read my manuscript in the hospice. It was the last piece of writing that she read.

Publishers I approached convinced me that I had something worth writing about but I had a lot further to go. So began the long road of writing, re-writing and editing. All feedback was taken seriously, and between exhibitions, arts writing and arts consultancy projects I kept developing the stories. I am grateful for the good advice in more recent years from Geoff Walker and Nadine Rubin Nathan.

My daughters Melina, Natalia, and Nikki, and my sister Eve, have been exceptional readers and critics, and I am ever grateful for their contributions. They catapulted me into re-working the fictional stories, many of which they recognized, into a factual version. Although other readers were less forthright, some recognized the similarity to my family's life.

My thanks go to Diana Wichtel, Sue Fisher, Ruth Busch, Linda Kaye, Sue Pezaro, Sonja Rosen, Gillian Taylor, Jane Legget, Ngaire Main and Sheridan Keith, some as readers and all in discussion – their support and encouragement kept me going.

Huge thanks go to Liesbeth Heenk of Amsterdam Publishers who agreed to publish my book, and I am most grateful to her for her feedback, trust, patience and support. On the verge of publishing, with her acceptance, I embarked on the process of stripping away the fictional imaginings that were based on kernels of truth and replaced them with real stories of my family's lives. This memoir, the 18 connected stories that I had been too afraid to write at the outset, became reality.

My reference material consisted mainly of recordings by my parents, which required a considerable amount of transcription. My sister Eve had commissioned interviews with Martha in the 1980s in the hope of making a film at that time. I am very grateful to Bob Weis who allowed us to have the original interviews conducted with Feliks for his documentary "Proud to Live".

Throughout the re-writing process Eve offered a layer of shared memories and editing that no one else could have provided. Her documentary film "Man on the Bus" (2019) led to unexpected information surfacing. My thanks go to journalist Greg Callahan, historian Waitman Beorn, Shaun Miller, Anatol Kark and the late Nina Zarel.

In September 2024, very unexpectedly, Maria Patro emailed Eve and me. She is the granddaughter of the family who provided refuge to our mother in Lvov during the war. Google led her to us – could we tell her more about her grandmother? The result has been a joyful exchange and I am very grateful for her curiosity and generous sharing of material that added to my research.

I couldn't have written this book without the ongoing loving support of my partner Michael Smythe and I thank him for his ongoing rigorous editing, persistence and design work. I am forever grateful.

ABOUT THE AUTHOR

Born in Poland, Helen Schamroth arrived in Melbourne with her parents in 1949 and has lived in Auckland, New Zealand since 1968. She has written extensively for national and international publications about craft and design, including her award-winning book "100 New Zealand Craft Artists". Her writing has evolved in parallel with her visual arts career, and she has exhibited nationally and internationally, including at the Triennale of Tapestry in Lodz, Poland. Working as an arts writer, arts consultant, curator and arts advocate, Helen has served on the Arts Board of Creative New Zealand and is a Life Member of the Designers' Institute of New Zealand. In 2005 she was made an Officer of the New Zealand Order of Merit for services to the arts.

AMSTERDAM PUBLISHERS HOLOCAUST LIBRARY

The series **Holocaust Survivor Memoirs World War II** consists of the following autobiographies of survivors:

Outcry. Holocaust Memoirs, by Manny Steinberg

Hank Brodt Holocaust Memoirs. A Candle and a Promise, by Deborah Donnelly

The Dead Years. Holocaust Memoirs, by Joseph Schupack

Rescued from the Ashes. The Diary of Leokadia Schmidt, Survivor of the Warsaw Ghetto, by Leokadia Schmidt

My Lvov. Holocaust Memoir of a twelve-year-old Girl, by Janina Hescheles

Remembering Ravensbrück. From Holocaust to Healing, by Natalie Hess

Wolf. A Story of Hate, by Zeev Scheinwald with Ella Scheinwald

Save my Children. An Astonishing Tale of Survival and its Unlikely Hero, by Leon Kleiner with Edwin Stepp

Holocaust Memoirs of a Bergen-Belsen Survivor & Classmate of Anne Frank, by Nanette Blitz Konig

Defiant German - Defiant Jew. A Holocaust Memoir from inside the Third Reich, by Walter Leopold with Les Leopold

In a Land of Forest and Darkness. The Holocaust Story of two Jewish Partisans, by Sara Lustigman Omelinski

Holocaust Memories. Annihilation and Survival in Slovakia, by Paul Davidovits

From Auschwitz with Love. The Inspiring Memoir of Two Sisters' Survival, Devotion and Triumph Told by Manci Grunberger Beran & Ruth Grunberger Mermelstein, by Daniel Seymour

Remetz. Resistance Fighter and Survivor of the Warsaw Ghetto, by Jan Yohay Remetz

My March Through Hell. A Young Girl's Terrifying Journey to Survival, by Halina Kleiner with Edwin Stepp

Roman's Journey, by Roman Halter

Beyond Borders. Escaping the Holocaust and Fighting the Nazis. 1938-1948, by Rudi Haymann

The Engineers. A memoir of survival through World War II in Poland and Hungary, by Henry Reiss

Spark of Hope. An Autobiography, by Luba Wrobel Goldberg

Footnote to History. From Hungary to America. The Memoir of a Holocaust Survivor, by Andrew Laszlo

Farewell Atlantis. Recollections, by Valentīna Freimane

The Courtyard. A memoir, by Benjamin Parket and Alexa Morris

The Mulberry Tree. The story of a life before and after the Holocaust, by Iboja Wandall-Holm

The Boy in the Back. A True Story of Survival in Auschwitz and Mauthausen, as told to Fern Lebo by Jan Blumenstein

Beneath the Lightless Sky. Surviving the Holocaust in the Sewers of Lvov, by Ignacy Chiger

Mendel Run, by Milton H. Schwartz

The series **Holocaust Survivor True Stories**
consists of the following biographies:

Among the Reeds. The true story of how a family survived the Holocaust, by Tammy Bottner

A Holocaust Memoir of Love & Resilience. Mama's Survival from Lithuania to America, by Ettie Zilber

Living among the Dead. My Grandmother's Holocaust Survival Story of Love and Strength, by Adena Bernstein Astrowsky

Heart Songs. A Holocaust Memoir, by Barbara Gilford

Shoes of the Shoah. The Tomorrow of Yesterday, by Dorothy Pierce

Hidden in Berlin. A Holocaust Memoir, by Evelyn Joseph Grossman

Separated Together. The Incredible True WWII Story of Soulmates Stranded an Ocean Apart, by Kenneth P. Price, Ph.D.

The Man Across the River. The incredible story of one man's will to survive the Holocaust, by Zvi Wiesenfeld

If Anyone Calls, Tell Them I Died. A Memoir, by Emanuel (Manu) Rosen

The House on Thrömerstrasse. A Story of Rebirth and Renewal in the Wake of the Holocaust, by Ron Vincent

Dancing with my Father. His hidden past. Her quest for truth. How Nazi Vienna shaped a family's identity, by Jo Sorochinsky

The Story Keeper. Weaving the Threads of Time and Memory - A Memoir, by Fred Feldman

Krisia's Silence. The Girl who was not on Schindler's List, by Ronny Hein

Defying Death on the Danube. A Holocaust Survival Story, by Debbie J. Callahan with Henry Stern

A Doorway to Heroism. A decorated German-Jewish Soldier who became an American Hero, by W. Jack Romberg

The Shoemaker's Son. The Life of a Holocaust Resister, by Laura Beth Bakst

The Redhead of Auschwitz. A True Story, by Nechama Birnbaum

Land of Many Bridges. My Father's Story, by Bela Ruth Samuel Tenenholtz

Creating Beauty from the Abyss. The Amazing Story of Sam Herciger, Auschwitz Survivor and Artist, by Lesley Ann Richardson

On Sunny Days We Sang. A Holocaust Story of Survival and Resilience, by Jeannette Grunhaus de Gelman

Painful Joy. A Holocaust Family Memoir, by Max J. Friedman

I Give You My Heart. A True Story of Courage and Survival, by Wendy Holden

In the Time of Madmen, by Mark A. Prelas

Monsters and Miracles. Horror, Heroes and the Holocaust, by Ira Wesley Kitmacher

Flower of Vlora. Growing up Jewish in Communist Albania, by Anna Kohen

Aftermath: Coming of Age on Three Continents. A Memoir, by Annette Libeskind Berkovits

Not a real Enemy. The True Story of a Hungarian Jewish Man's Fight for Freedom, by Robert Wolf

Zaidy's War. Four Armies, Three Continents, Two Brothers. One Man's Impossible Story of Endurance, by Martin Bodek

The Glassmaker's Son. Looking for the World my Father left behind in Nazi Germany, by Peter Kupfer

The Apprentice of Buchenwald. The True Story of the Teenage Boy Who Sabotaged Hitler's War Machine, by Oren Schneider

Good for a Single Journey, by Helen Joyce

Burying the Ghosts. She escaped Nazi Germany only to have her life torn apart by the woman she saved from the camps: her mother, by Sonia Case

American Wolf. From Nazi Refugee to American Spy. A True Story, by Audrey Birnbaum

Bipolar Refugee. A Saga of Survival and Resilience, by Peter Wiesner

In the Wake of Madness. My Family's Escape from the Nazis, by Bettie Lennett Denny

Before the Beginning and After the End, by Hymie Anisman

I Will Give Them an Everlasting Name. Jacksonville's Stories of the Holocaust, by Samuel Cox

Hiding in Holland. A Resistance Memoir, by Shulamit Reinharz

The Ghosts on the Wall. A Grandson's Memoir of the Holocaust, by Kenneth D. Wald

Thirteen in Auschwitz. My grandmother's fight to stay human, by Lauren Meyerowitz Port

The Jewish Woman Who Fought the Nazis. Bep Schaap-Bedak's life during the Holocaust in Holland, by Eli Schaap

Voices of Resilience. An Anthology of Stories written by Children of Holocaust Survivors, Edited by Deborah (Devora) Ross-Grayman

Dreaming of the River, by Pauline Steinhorn

The series **Jewish Children in the Holocaust** consists of the following autobiographies of Jewish children hidden during WWII in the Netherlands:

Searching for Home. The Impact of WWII on a Hidden Child, by Joseph Gosler

Sounds from Silence. Reflections of a Child Holocaust Survivor, Psychiatrist and Teacher, by Robert Krell

Sabine's Odyssey. A Hidden Child and her Dutch Rescuers, by Agnes Schipper

The Journey of a Hidden Child,

by Harry Pila and Robin Black

The series **New Jewish Fiction** consists of the following novels, written by Jewish authors. All novels are set in the time during or after the Holocaust.

The Corset Maker. A Novel, by Annette Libeskind Berkovits

Escaping the Whale. The Holocaust is over. But is it ever over for the next generation? by Ruth Rotkowitz

When the Music Stopped. Willy Rosen's Holocaust, by Casey Hayes

Hands of Gold. One Man's Quest to Find the Silver Lining in Misfortune, by Roni Robbins

The Girl Who Counted Numbers. A Novel, by Roslyn Bernstein

There was a garden in Nuremberg. A Novel, by Navina Michal Clemerson

The Butterfly and the Axe, by Omer Bartov

To Live Another Day. A Novel, by Elizabeth Rosenberg

The Right to Happiness. After all they went through. Stories, by Helen Schary Motro

Five Amber Beads, by Richard Aronowitz

To Love Another Day. A Novel, by Elizabeth Rosenberg

Cursing the Darkness. A Novel about Loss and Recovery, by Joanna Rosenthall

The series **Holocaust Heritage** consists of the following memoirs by 2G:

The Cello Still Sings. A Generational Story of the Holocaust and of the Transformative Power of Music, by Janet Horvath

The Fire and the Bonfire. A Journey into Memory, by Ardyn Halter

The Silk Factory: Finding Threads of My Family's True Holocaust Story, by Michael Hickins

Winter Light. The Memoir of a Child of Holocaust Survivors, by Grace Feuerverger

Out from the Shadows. Growing up with Holocaust Survivor Parents, by Willie Handler

Hidden in Plain Sight. A Family Memoir and the Untold Story of the Holocaust in Serbia, by Julie Brill

The Unspeakable. Breaking my family's silence surrounding the Holocaust, by Nicola Hanefeld

Eighteen for Life. Surviving the Holocaust,

by Helen Schamroth

Four Survivor Grandparents. Run. Rely. Rebuild, by Jonathan Schloss

Austrian Again. Reclaiming a Lost Legacy,

by Anne Hand

The series **Holocaust Books for Young Adults** consists of the following novels, based on true stories:

The Boy behind the Door. How Salomon Kool Escaped the Nazis. Inspired by a True Story, by David Tabatsky

Running for Shelter. A True Story, by Suzette Sheft

The Precious Few. An Inspirational Saga of Courage based on True Stories, by David Twain with Art Twain

Dark Shadows Hover, by Jordan Steven Sher

The Sun will Shine Again, by Cynthia Goldstein Monsour

The Memory Place. How My Parents Survived 17 Concentration Camps, by Monica van Rijn

The series **WWII Historical Fiction** consists of the following novels, some of which are based on true stories:

Mendelevski's Box. A Heartwarming and Heartbreaking Jewish Survivor's Story, by Roger Swindells

A Quiet Genocide. The Untold Holocaust of Disabled Children in WWII Germany, by Glenn Bryant

The Knife-Edge Path, by Patrick T. Leahy

Brave Face. The Inspiring WWII Memoir of a Dutch/German Child, by I. Caroline Crocker and Meta A. Evenbly

When We Had Wings. The Gripping Story of an Orphan in Janusz Korczak's Orphanage. A Historical Novel, by Tami Shem-Tov

Jacob's Courage. Romance and Survival amidst the Horrors of War, by Charles S. Weinblatt

A Semblance of Justice. Based on true Holocaust experiences, by Wolf Holles

Under the Pink Triangle. Where forbidden love meets unspeakable evil, by Katie Moore

Amsterdam Publishers Newsletter

Subscribe to our Newsletter by selecting the menu at the top (right) of **amsterdampublishers.com**

www.ingramcontent.com/pod-product-compliance
Lightning Source LLC
LaVergne TN
LVHW041922070526
838199LV00051BA/2700
9789493418257